I0748873

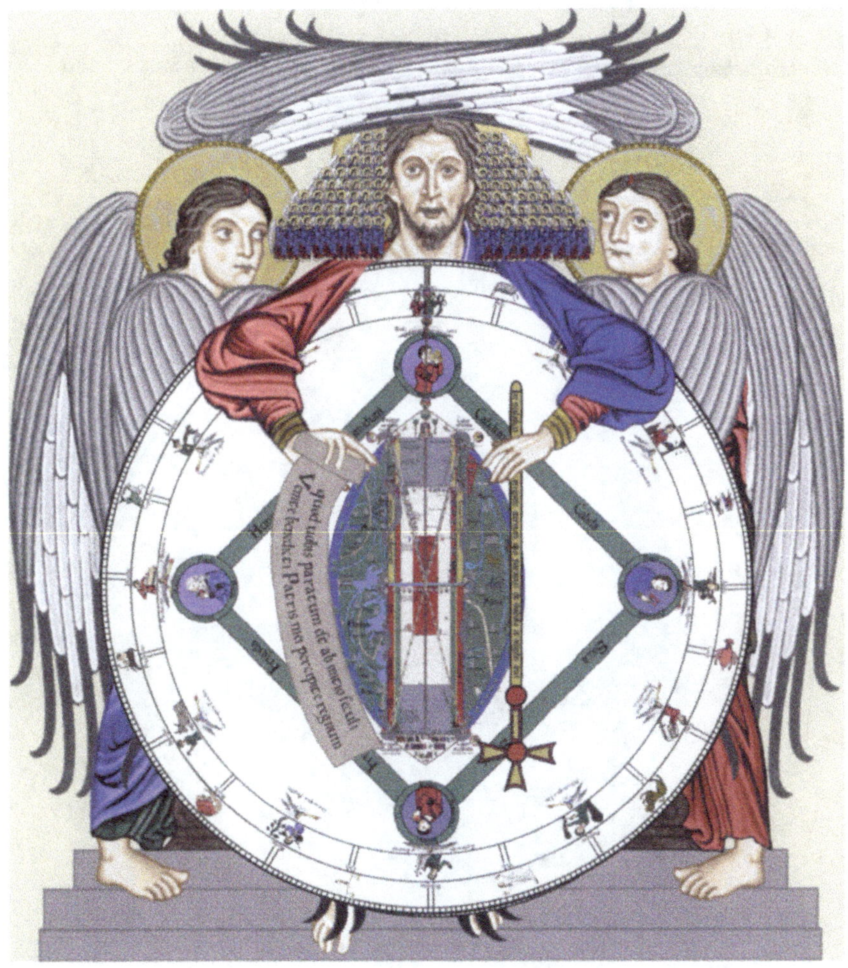

Fig. 1. *The Mystic Ark* as it might have appeared if constructed at the convent of Hohenbourg during the abbacy of Abbess Herrad in the late twelfth century. Digital reconstruction, Clement/Han/Rudolph.

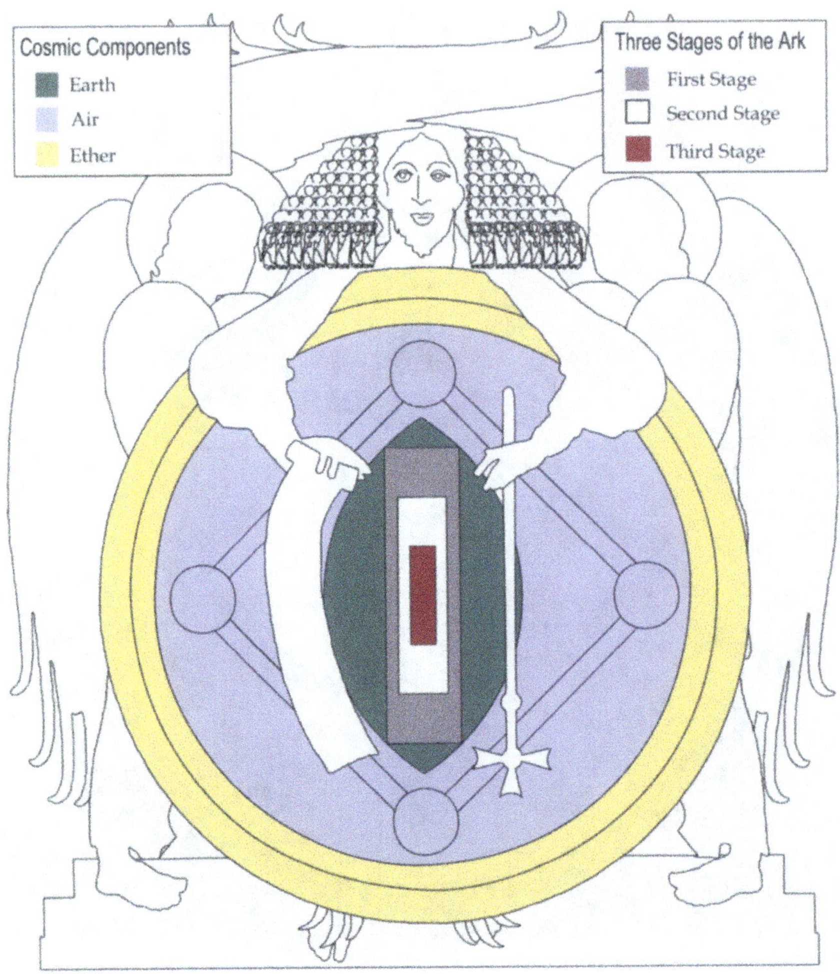

Fig. 4. *The Mystic Ark.* Earth, air, ether, and the three stages. Clement/Rudolph.

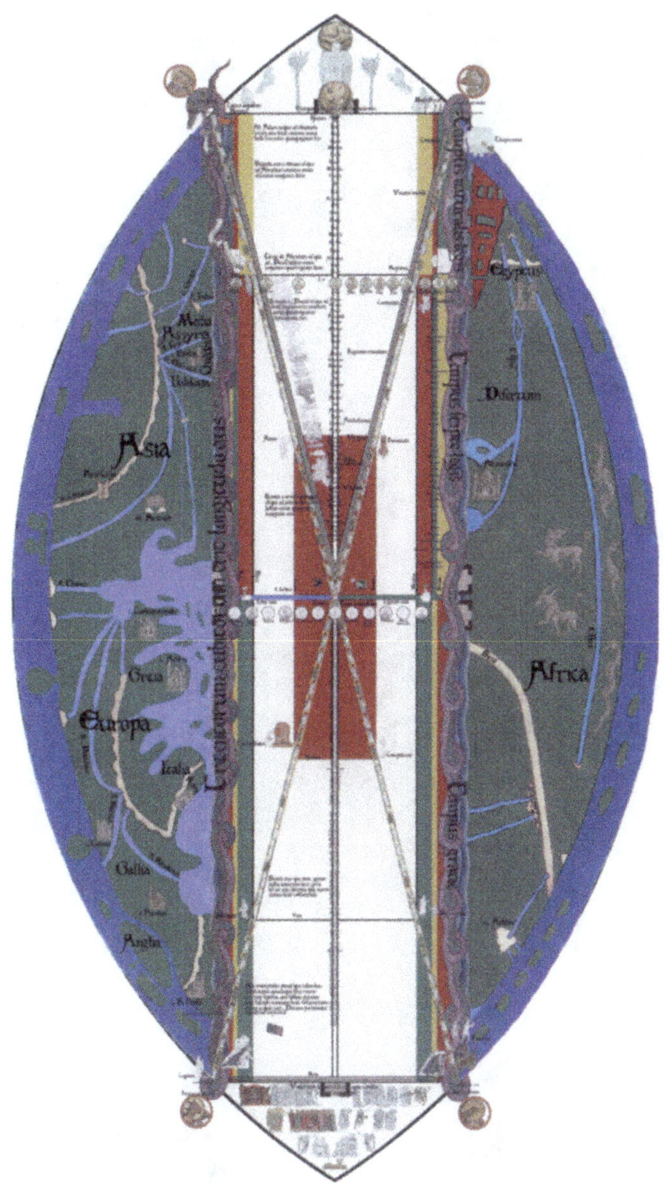

Fig. 5. *The Mystic Ark.* Selected components of the Ark and earth. Clement/Rudolph.

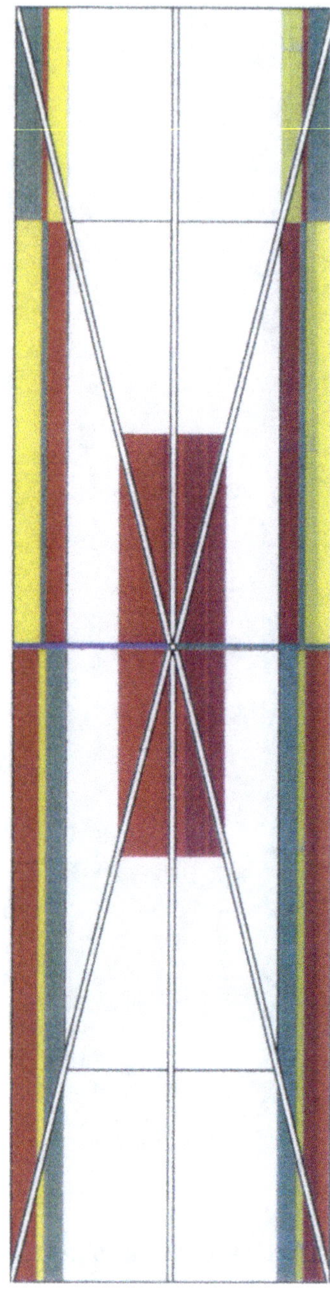

Fig. 8. *The Mystic Ark*. The four ascents. Clement/Rudolph.

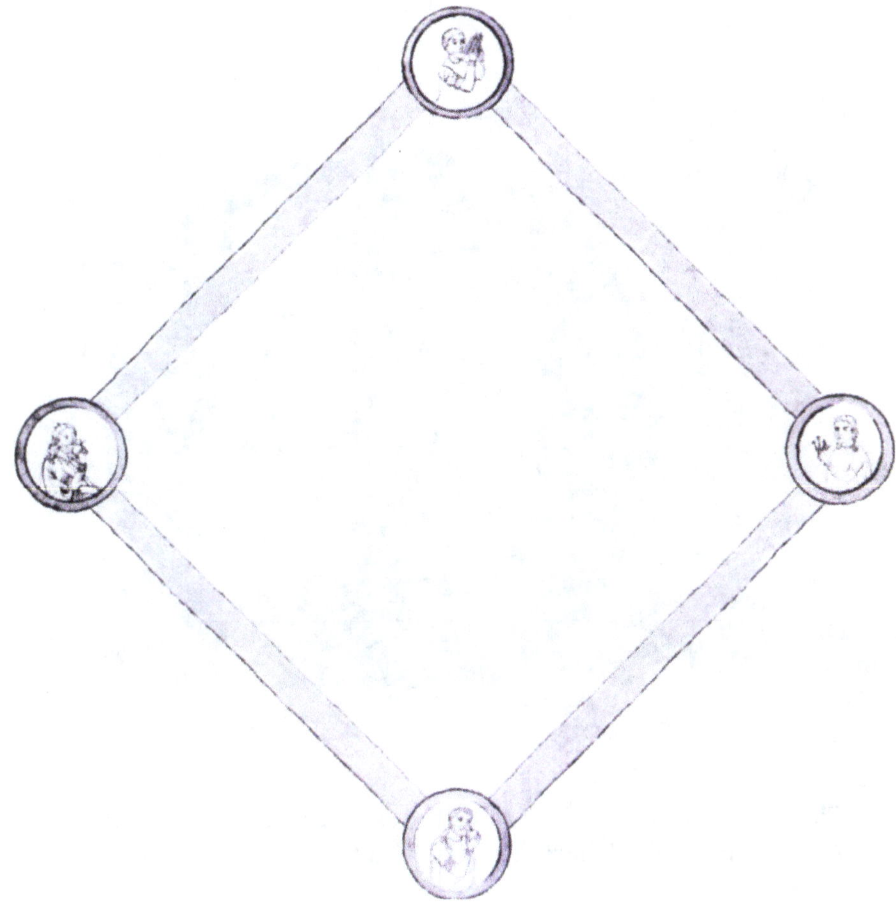

Fig. 9. *The Mystic Ark*. Quaternary harmony. Clement/Rudolph.

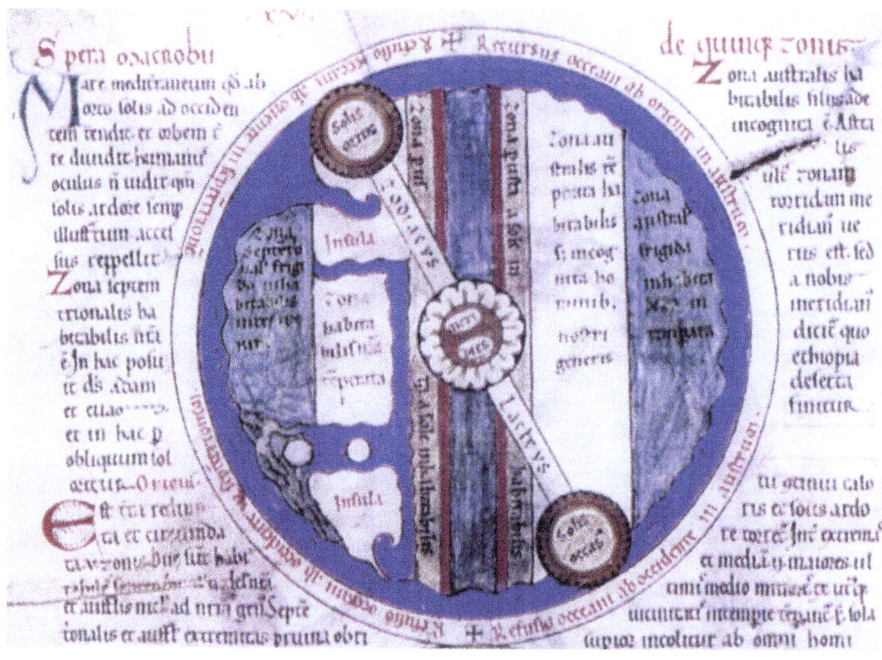

Fig. 12. *Sphera Macrobii*. Lambert of Saint-Omer, *Liber Floridus*. Herzog August Bibliothek Wolfenbüttel, Ms. 1 Gud. lat. fol. 16v.

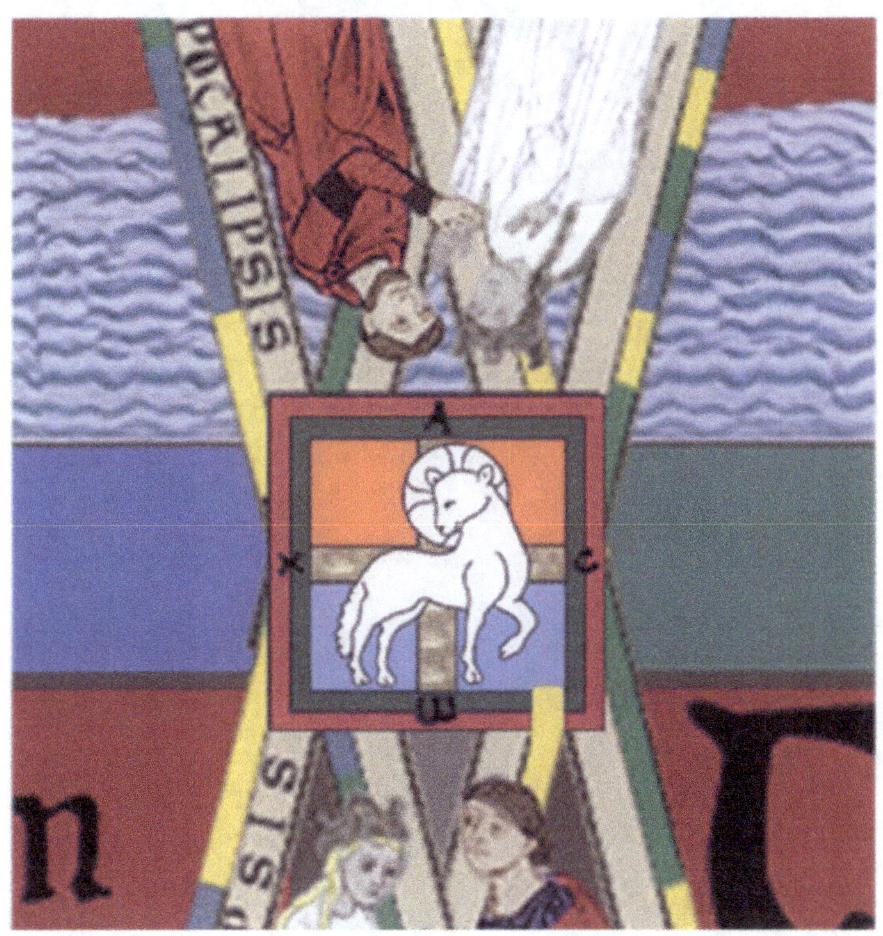

Fig. 13. *The Mystic Ark*. The central cubit. Clement/Rudolph.

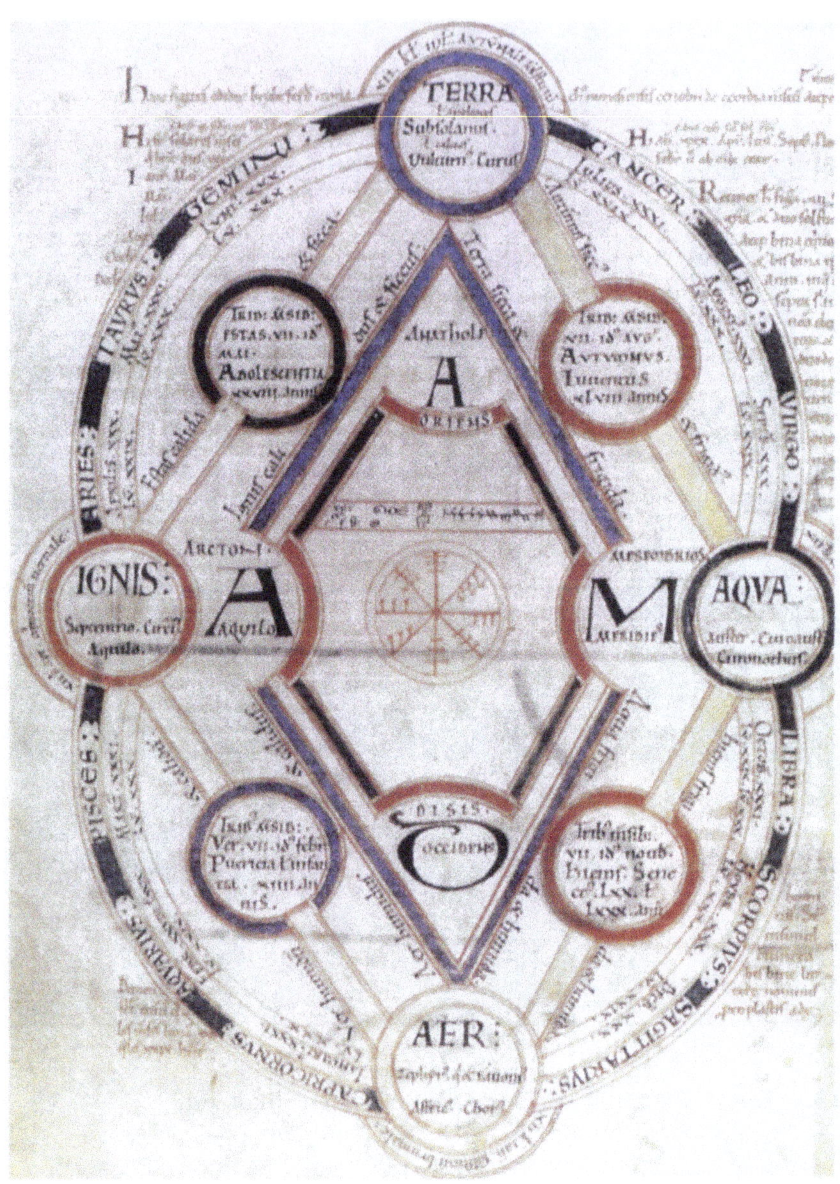

Fig. 14. Macro/microcosm (Byrhtferth's Diagram). The President and Scholars of Saint John Baptist College in the University of Oxford, Ms. 17:7v.

TRANSACTIONS
of the
AMERICAN PHILOSOPHICAL SOCIETY
Held at Philadelphia
For Promoting Useful Knowledge
Volume 94, Part 4

"FIRST, I FIND THE CENTER POINT": READING THE TEXT OF HUGH OF SAINT VICTOR'S *THE MYSTIC ARK*

Conrad Rudolph

American Philosophical Society
Philadelphia • 2004

ISBN: 0-87169-944-3
US ISSN: 0065-9746

Library of Congress Cataloging-in-Publication Data

Rudolph, Conrad, 1951–
First, I find the center point : reading the text of Hugh of Saint Victor's The mystic ark / Conrad Rudolph.
p. cm. — (Transactions of the American Philosophical Society ; v. 94, pt. 4)
Includes bibliographical references and index.
ISBN 0-87169-944-3 (paper)
1. Christian art and symbolism—France—Medieval, 500–1500. 2. Theology—Early works to 1800. 3. Hugh, of Saint-Victor, 1096?–1141. Mystic ark (Painting) 4. Hugh, of Saint-Victor, 1096?–1141—Criticism and interpretation. 5. Mysticism in art. 6. Lost works of art—France. I. Hugh, of Saint-Victor, 1096?–1141. De arca Noe mystica. II. Title. III. Series.

N7850.R78 2004
704.9'484—dc22

2004054542

To the memory of Robert Benson
1925–1996
professor of medieval history,
colleague, and friend

CONTENTS

Color Plates for Figures 1, 4, 5, 8, 9, 12, 13 and 14 appear in the front of the book

PREFACE

"First, I find the center point on the surface where I wish to depict the Ark, and there—the point having been fixed—I draw a small square centered on it in the likeness of that cubit in which the Ark was brought to completion." With these words begins perhaps the most unusual source we have for the history of medieval art, Hugh of Saint Victor's *The Mystic Ark*. Seemingly straightforward enough, the seeds of two serious misconceptions about the *Ark* are inherent in this opening passage and, indeed, throughout the text of *The Mystic Ark*. These are that Hugh himself was the actual writer of the text of *The Mystic Ark* and that this text is an actual step-by-step set of instructions for the production of the painting of *The Mystic Ark*.

These misconceptions have been with us from the beginning of modern scholarship on the *Ark*. In trying to come to terms with them as part of a larger study of mine on the subject, it became apparent that there were a number of other, equally misleading views that, for the most part, have appeared with the great increase in interest in *The Mystic Ark* over the last dozen or so years. These address such essential issues as the relation between the painting and the text of *The Mystic Ark*; the relation between the text of *The Mystic Ark* and *The Moral Ark* (a related treatise by Hugh); why a second recension of *The Mystic Ark* was made; the significance of the slight differences between the two recensions; whether the text is a work of ekphrasis; whether it was meant to serve as a substitute for an image that was too difficult to produce and preserve; whether *The Mystic Ark* was ever painted; whether it was intended to be painted by others; and so on.

These questions must be asked if we want to have a comprehensive understanding of the text and image of *The Mystic Ark*. But the body of responses to them, as they now stand, have distorted our current view of *The Mystic Ark* to such a degree that it is impossible to have a clear sense of this important source without first reexamining the textual basis of these issues. This is not an easy task. Both the text and the image of the *Ark* are so complex that neither subject can be dealt with in anything approaching an effective manner in the same work. Therefore, before taking up the image of *The Mystic Ark* in its own right, something I will do in a later study, the nature of the *Ark* as a written text must first be examined more carefully. In doing this, I believe that, as *The Mystic Ark* becomes better understood and better known, it will take its place alongside Bernard of Clairvaux's *Apologia* and the writings of Suger of Saint-Denis as one of the best means we have for stripping away the clouded varnish of history to reveal ever more of the extraordinarily vibrant artistic culture of early twelfth-century Europe, an artistic culture that was nowhere more active—both in utilizing imagery and in cautioning against its use—than among the well-educated and intellectually sophisticated members of the often wealthy leading houses of the monastic and collegial orders.

*
* *

Though it is not a long work, I have incurred many debts in the course of writing this study. On the basis of time alone, thanks must be made first to the John Simon Guggenheim Foundation for their assistance in the overall project, of which this book is just a part; the Foundation has a sense, but cannot ever fully know, I believe, how the moral support that its fellows receive from them outweighs their generous financial support. Related and deeply felt thanks must also go to Kurt Forster, Herb Kessler, John Williams, and the much missed Robert Benson.

The digitally produced image, which will appear in a more detailed way in my later study of the image of the *Ark*, has been a major project in itself. In my complete dependence, I am grateful to Karen Genet, Madelyn Millen, Leo Schouest, Sohail Wassif, and Ben Han, who was the first digital artist of this project. My gratitude to the second artist, Claire Clement, a person of unlimited generosity and talent, knows no bounds; the production of the image of *The Mystic Ark* would not have been possible without her skill and dedication. Even so, it is unlikely that there would have been any images at all without the generous financial and moral support of, first, Emory Elliott, Director of the Center for Ideas and Society at the University of California, Riverside, and, later, Lisa Ackerman of the Samuel H. Kress Foundation. I am deeply indebted to both of these people and institutions. I am equally indebted to Michelle Brown, Max Neiman, and John Williams (again) for their help along these lines. I also thank Mieke Bahmer, who made the three-dimensional reconstruction of *The Mystic Ark* that appears in this study, an image that goes a long way in helping those who are new to the *Ark* understand its structure as expressed in the two-dimensional painting.

Gratitude must be expressed to Steven Ostrow for his much-appreciated critical reading of the manuscript, and to Dan Sheerin for his invaluable advice on the translation of *The Mystic Ark*, which will appear in my later study. My sincere appreciation goes as well to Julia Bloomfield, Sara Chan, Judson Emerick, Françoise Forster-Hahn, John Ganim, Stephen Gersh, Cornelius O'Boyle, and Marina Smyth for a wide variety of help and support related to this project, and to Paul Binski and Christian Heck, among others already mentioned, for their support in general. Finally, very special thanks are owed to Mark Jordan and Glenn Olsen for their thoughtful readings and suggestions as press readers.

Readers are advised to be aware of the distinction between my use of "the Ark," by which I mean the iconographical component of the Ark proper in the image of *The Mystic Ark*, and "the *Ark*," a shortened title I sometimes use when referring to either the image or the text of *The Mystic Ark*.

This book is dedicated to the memory of Robert Benson, 1925–1996, professor of medieval history, colleague, and friend.

Introduction

Perhaps nowhere in medieval culture do art, science, and theology better converge than in Hugh of Saint Victor's *The Mystic Ark*, a work that was conceived, not coincidentally, at a moment of previously unrivalled controversy over art and of perceived threat by science to theology. The time was one of enormous social, intellectual, and political change; change in which the emerging and often contentious schools of Europe played a central role, particularly in the crucial areas of science and the systematization of theology. *The Mystic Ark* is the name of both a painting made by Hugh for the school of Saint Victor and the text that describes it, the two being created sometime from 1125 to early 1130. It was no accident that it was from within this highly charged and itself radically changing world of the education of the intellectual elite that *The Mystic Ark* originated.

Despite the vast body of writings left by Hugh, very little is known of his life in general and even less of his early life in particular. But there is just enough to make it possible to construct a basic outline of his life, a context, however sketchy, in which his work and thought can be understood. Hugh was born sometime in the late eleventh century, probably in Saxony, and is believed to have been educated there by the canons regular of Hamersleben. Around 1115 he entered the abbey of Saint Victor, a house of canons regular, at that time just on the eastern edge of Left Bank Paris. By 1133, he had become master of the school there, chosen for this office at a time when the schools were expanding dramatically in size and importance. The school of Saint Victor was among the most renowned, particularly while under his direction. The house of Saint Victor was deeply involved in the reform of the secular Church in northern France, and Hugh himself was active in contemporary intellectual politics through his position as a teacher and a scholar. By the time of his death in early 1141, his teaching and writings were such that he was considered by many to be the leading theologian in Western Europe during the mid-twelfth century, one of the great moments of European intellectual history, even being called *alter Augustinus,* a second Augustine, by his contemporaries.[1]

Together, the painting and text of *The Mystic Ark* form one of the most unusual sources we have for an understanding of medieval visual culture and its polemical context. The painting—the most complex single work of figural art from the entire Middle Ages—is known to have served as the focal point of a series of brilliant and highly political lectures undertaken by the great theologian Hugh at Saint Victor (Fig. 1). The equally exceptional text provides a description of this image that is no less than forty-one and a quarter pages long in the modern critical edition: the longest description of a single actual work of figural art from the Middle Ages proper by around forty-one pages. The text was meant to aid in the repeated production of the image (although it is not an actual step-by-

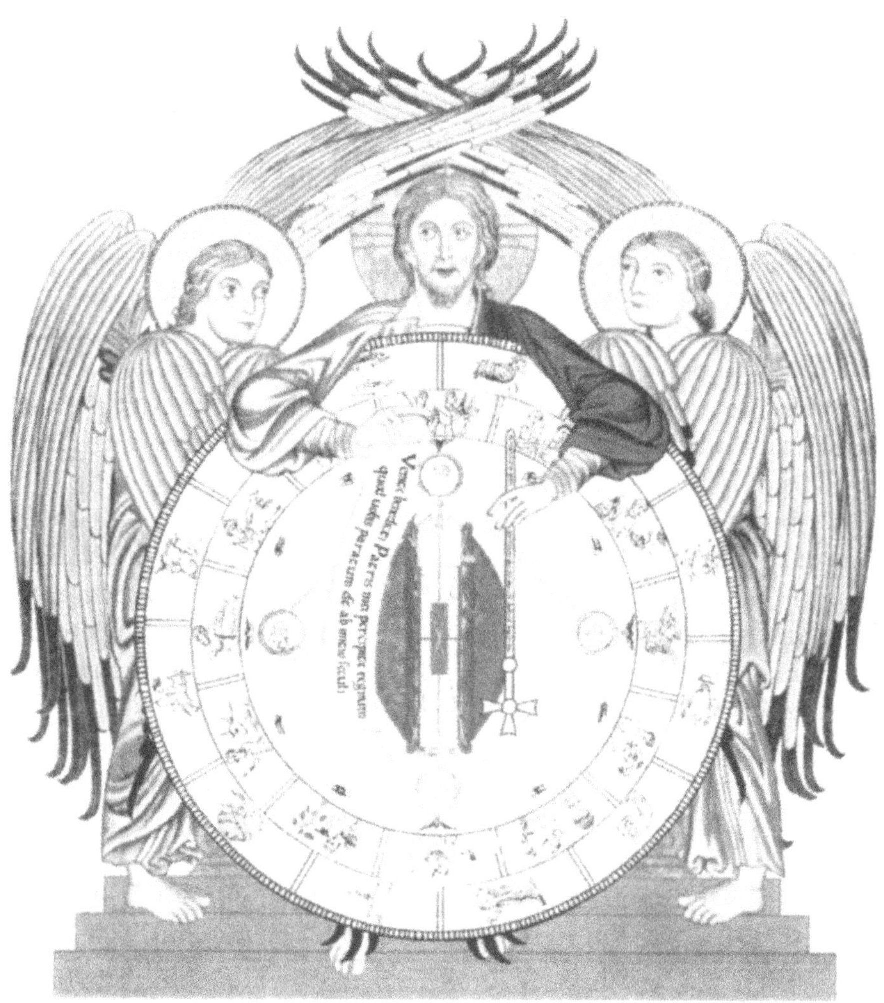

Fig. 1. *The Mystic Ark* as it might have appeared if constructed at the convent of Hohenbourg during the abbacy of Abbess Herrad in the late twelfth century. Digital reconstruction, Clement/Han/Rudolph.

step set of instructions), each production, in a sense, being an "original." But the importance of *The Mystic Ark* for the history of medieval art extends beyond the *Ark* itself. For Hugh acted as an advisor to Abbot Suger on his famous art program at Saint-Denis.[2] And, with or without the direct guidance of Hugh on this particular point, the systematization of imagery in *The Mystic Ark* seems to have served as the impetus to the systematization of imagery in the west portals of Saint-Denis, the first fully systematized, the first Gothic, portals constructed (Fig. 3).

The painting of *The Mystic Ark* presents an elaborate visual summary of the entire history of salvation—in a religious sense, all of human history that matters—from the beginning until the end of time, pointedly in association with all of creation, both spiritual and physical, and under divine dispensation. Imposed on top of this universal history and fully integrated with it is a complex schema of individual salvation that is also related to the salvation of humankind as a whole.

More specifically, the painting effects its meaning through the depiction of Christ embracing the cosmos, with the six days of creation proceeding from his mouth. The cosmos is composed of the three cosmic zones of ether, air, and earth, all of which is heavily dependent on figural forms found in the traditions of pedagogic schemata (Figs. 2 and 4). The zone of ether is indicated by the representations of the Twelve Signs of the Zodiac and the Twelve Months, arranged in two concentric rings. In the region of air, the Twelve Winds are portrayed along with a rather complete quaternary harmony. Through the earth—fully represented as a *mappa mundi,* itself a major vehicle for Hugh's theoretical views on the history of salvation—the Chosen People are shown, first wandering from Egypt to the Promised Land, and then being dragged off into captivity in Babylon (Fig. 5, no. 18, 19). Symbolically coterminous with the earth, an image of the Ark of Noah is the focus of this complex composition, an image that is meant to be understood as holding four exegetically distinct readings as the Ark of Noah, the Ark of the Church, the Ark of Wisdom, and the Ark of Mother Grace. The component of the Ark is far too involved to be described here, except to say that it is composed of three stages that are meant to be understood as projecting three-dimensionally toward the viewer (Figs. 4 and 6). Ladders rise up from each of the Ark's four corners, up which sixty men and sixty women climb toward the Lamb of God in the central cubit in which the Ark culminates, according to Genesis 6:16 (Fig. 5, no. 7–10, 1). Throughout all this, hundreds of figures, symbols, and inscriptions operate—from the creation of humankind to the Last Judgment—typically at an astonishingly high degree of coordination.

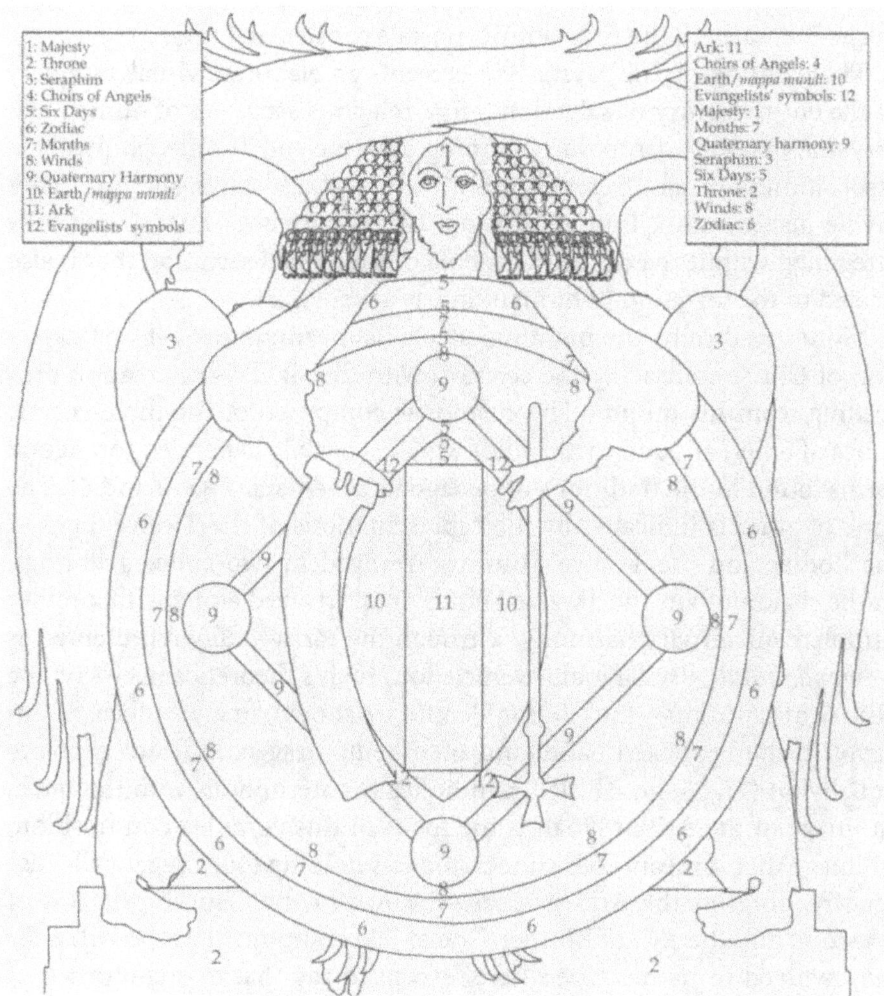

Fig. 2. *The Mystic Ark*, selected major components. Clement/Rudolph.

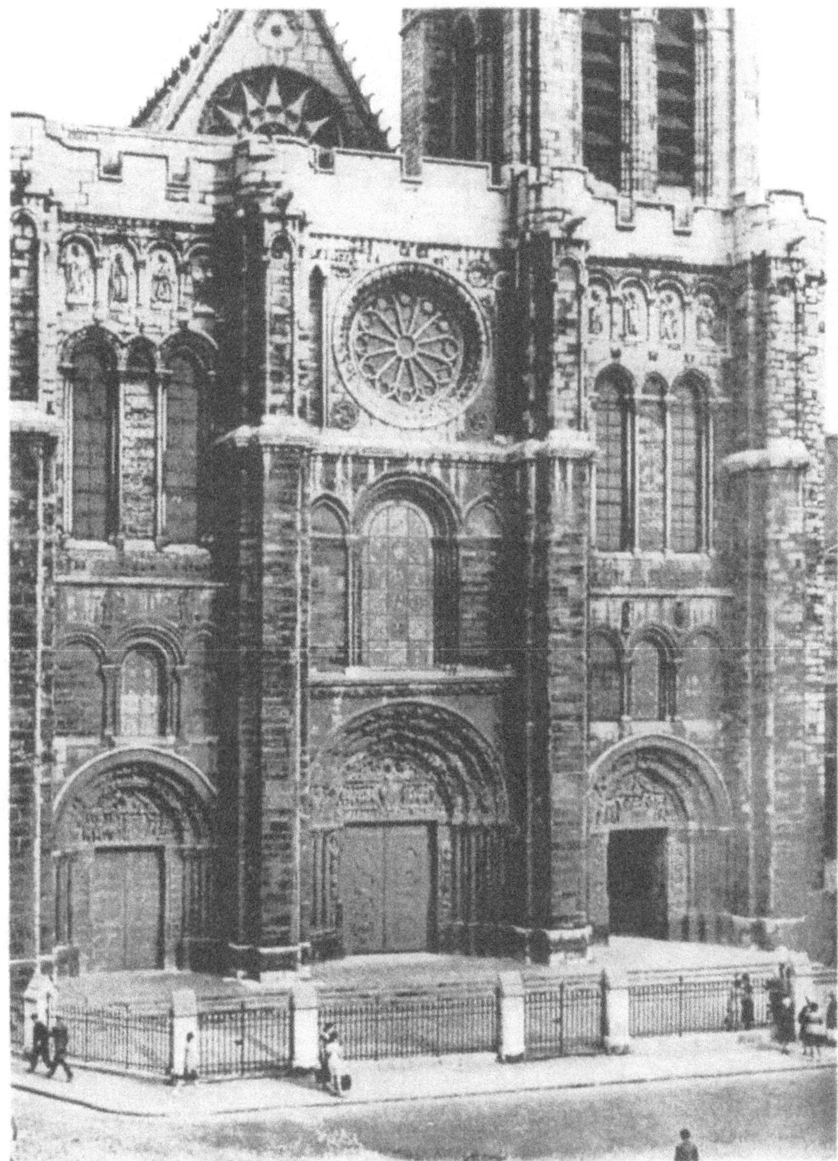

Fig. 3. Saint-Denis, west portals (photo Gueiroard).

Fundamentally political, *The Mystic Ark* constitutes a major statement on the history of salvation phrased in a very specific way, one that addresses the contemporarily important issues of creation, systematic theology, neoplatonism, and the place of science in the education of society's intellectual elite.[3] The purpose of the painting was to present these issues in an integrated visual format that could serve as the focal point for extensive discussions of the issues. The purpose of the text was to enable

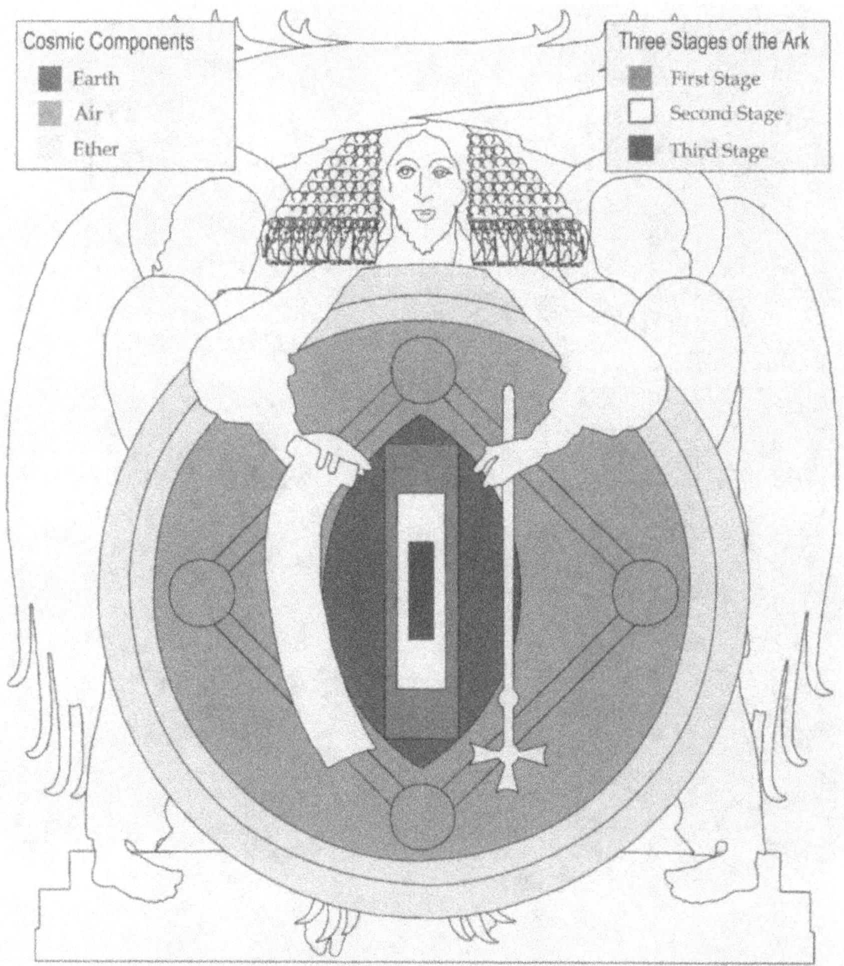

Fig. 4. *The Mystic Ark.* Earth, air, ether, and the three stages. Clement/Rudolph.

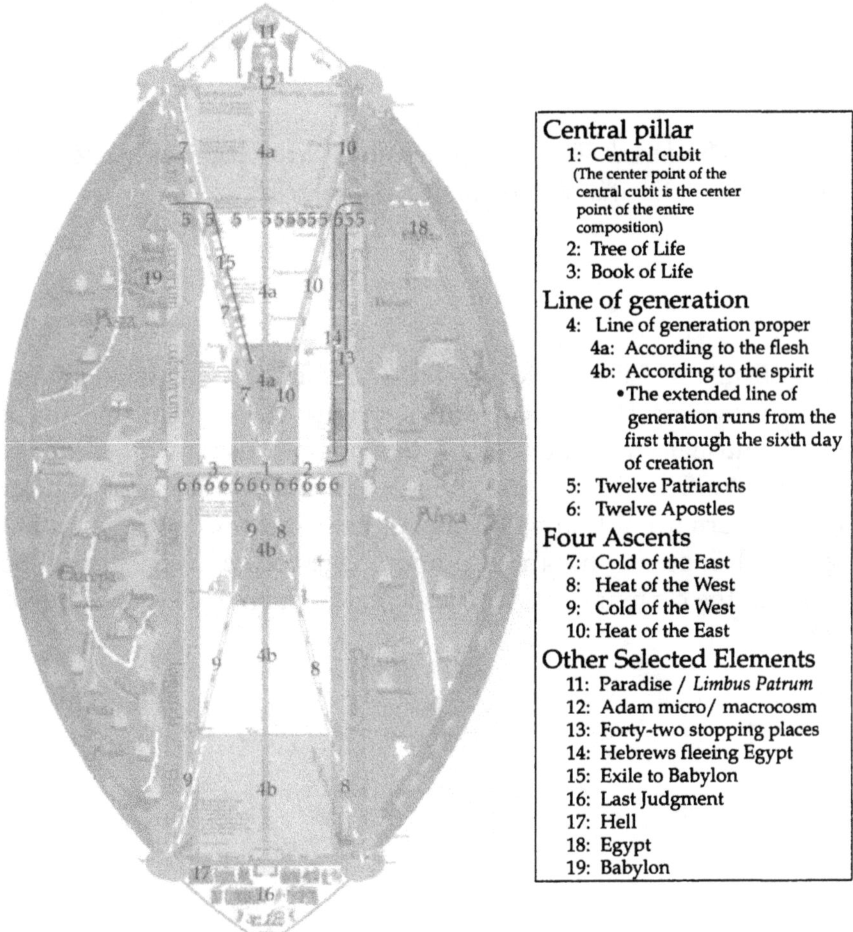

Fig. 5. *The Mystic Ark.* Selected components of the Ark and earth. Clement/Rudolph.

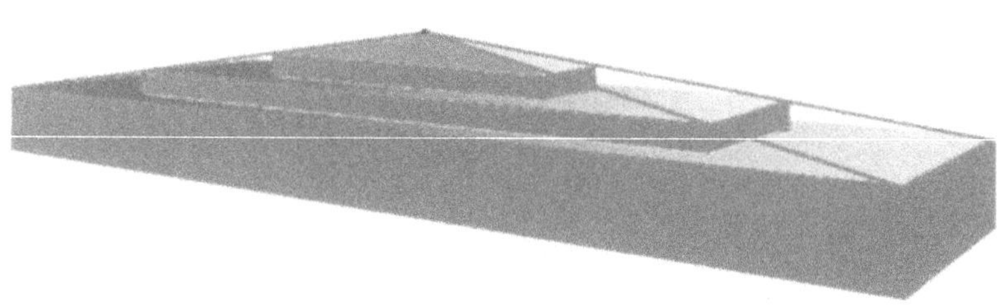

Fig. 6. *The Mystic Ark.* The two-dimensional Ark proper projected into three dimensions. Digital reconstruction Bahmer/Rudolph.

scholars outside of Saint Victor to undertake similar discussions themselves by providing the information necessary to produce the image. Given the unusually large number of surviving manuscript copies of *The Mystic Ark* (enough to make it as popular as some of the most popular writings by Bernard of Clairvaux, arguably the most widely read author of the time[4]), it seems that the text and image played a very active and novel role in the current controversies with which Hugh was concerned.

Chapter One

THE TEXT OF *THE MYSTIC ARK* AS A *REPORTATIO*

In one of his fictive moral letters to Lucilius, Seneca, the genuinely amoral Roman statesman and philosopher, wrote, "It is necessary that you pay close attention—and blame the difficulty of these things on Plato, not on me!"[5] I could easily say the same thing about Hugh of Saint Victor with regard to *The Mystic Ark*, a text so difficult to read and to understand that its very difficulty seems to be the reason why it has previously been almost completely ignored by art historians.

But this would be unfair to Hugh—or at least a little unfair. For, despite what can only be described as a horrific text, equal blame must be shared with modern scholars. Indeed, just as scholars used to wonder how such a disorderly thinker as Abbot Suger of Saint-Denis could have conceived such orderly artworks, so some of them still wonder how such an orderly thinker as Hugh could have produced such a disorderly text as *The Mystic Ark*, the written expression of the supremely orderly image of *The Mystic Ark*. In an earlier study, I showed how the order in some of Suger's artworks was the result of Hugh's role as a principal advisor to Suger on his art program.[6] It can now also be shown that the disorderliness of the text of *The Mystic Ark* is owed to the fact that the text is not by Hugh per se but is a *reportatio*: while the intellectual, visual, and oral images of *The Mystic Ark* are or were by Hugh, the main body of the text of *The Mystic Ark* was not actually written by Hugh himself, but by an anonymous reporter as something similar to lecture notes, although Hugh remains its author, morally speaking.

Having failed to make this fundamental observation, scholars have in many cases needlessly compounded the difficulties of this tortuous writing with equally tortuous explanations, hoping to force the round pegs of the evidence into the square holes of their preconceived arguments. Twisting and turning more than the serpentine attribute of a medieval personification of Dialectic, these arguments have such potential for causing confusion that it is only by addressing them individually that a coherent view of this complex text can be presented and "the difficulty of these things" kept to a minimum.

On the basis of both a passage in *The Mystic Ark* that refers to *The Moral Ark* as already written and a number of references in *The Moral Ark* that speak of the painting of *The Mystic Ark* as preexistent, the traditional view has been simply that *The Moral Ark* was written first and that *The Mystic Ark* was then written in order to describe the painting of the ark-schema that is referred to in *The Moral Ark*. Although this order of composition may be correct as far as it goes, most scholars have ignored the greater significance of these same references in *The Moral Ark* to the preexistent painting and the actual relation between the painting of *The Mystic Ark*, the treatise of *The Moral Ark*, and the text of *The Mystic Ark*, and none have seriously questioned why the text of *The Mystic Ark* should be so unlike Hugh's other writings in its lack of clarity.

In a pair of, at times, contradictory studies on Hugh and *The Mystic Ark*, Patrice Sicard, a canon regular, has attempted to go further than those before him in trying to articulate the origins of the painting and text of *The Mystic Ark* and their relation to *The Moral Ark*.[7] Despite a great deal of very useful and much-appreciated work, Sicard makes two basic errors of interpretation that fundamentally affect the vast majority of his extended analysis of the subject. The first is his lack of recognition that the text of *The Mystic Ark* is a *reportatio*.[8]

1. FIRST SUGGESTIONS OF THE TEXT OF *THE MYSTIC ARK* AS A *REPORTATIO*

The initial obstacle in coming to an understanding of the nature and function of the text of *The Mystic Ark* immediately presents itself in the absence of any introductory statement regarding its purpose, a statement it very much needs. With no preface whatsoever, the text begins abruptly in the first person (the voice of Hugh) and proceeds in a very uneven series of seemingly practical instructions for the production of the painting of *The Mystic Ark*: now being very methodical, now adopting a sermon-like quality, now slipping into an irredeemably laconic tone, toward the end seemingly losing interest in the undertaking, and finally concluding with a very brief statement on the function of the text that is something less than illuminating.

As discussed below, the text is on occasion unclear or even confused; it is filled with inconsistencies; it often gets ahead of its own description, taking for granted information that has not yet been introduced; and it displays a weak knowledge of the Bible at times—to name only a few of the problems that arise from this work. This is entirely out of keeping with Hugh's other writings, which display a high degree of clarity, consistency, logic in the order of information introduced, biblical knowledge, and general enthusiasm for the subject at hand.[9] With a few isolated exceptions, the only consistent stylistic element that the text of *The Mystic Ark* has in common with the body of Hugh's writings is the high level of its basic organization, something that stems directly from the very nature of the painting and that is at times severely strained in the written presentation when the text moves away from the structural logic of the painting. As any university professor will confirm, all of these traits of the text of *The Mystic Ark* are fully in character with student notes of a complex lecture.

While the term "*reportatio*" does not appear before the thirteenth century, the practice of a reporter taking notes during an oral presentation in a class situation is one found throughout the Middle Ages.[10] As described by Beryl Smalley, a *reportatio* is not exactly class notes, but rather something like class notes worked into a fuller state, sometimes put into the first person, typically for the use of others. Though it may be recopied again and again without recomposition, it may need to be corrected and to have references supplied. Above all, it has no pretensions to literature.[11]

Not only did Hugh actively participate in the making of *reportationes*, but the first detailed account of the practice comes from his very lectures. In the *Sententie de divinitate* of around 1127 (precisely the same time as the *Ark* lectures), a student named Laurence, perhaps later abbot of Westminster, describes his own experience in the process of making a *reportatio* of a series of lectures by Hugh that presents an early, oral form of a portion of the first part of Hugh's *De sacramentis*.[12] According to Laurence,

> I brought my tablets [of worked-up notes of the lecture] back to Master Hugh once a week so that, under his direction, if there were anything superfluous it might be cut out, anything overlooked might be added, anything poorly phrased might be changed.[13]

Even so, he put the lectures into a language that was very simple and ultimately his own, like lecture notes today. The same can be said for another *reportatio* of Hugh's lectures, the *Descriptio mappe mundi*, where the writing is again in a very simple style. This piece, however, also has a preface written in a literary style that is in such stark contrast to the body of the work as to suggest that the two were written by different persons, with the prologue in all probability being by Hugh himself.[14] In contrast, the irregularity of the writing of the text traditionally ascribed to Hugh and known as *De contemplatione* has suggested that it was a *reportatio* that was assembled by a student reporter without Hugh having revised or even reviewed it.[15] Thus, while all of these writings are *reportationes* of Hugh's lectures, the degree to which Hugh participated in them varied: in the first, Hugh followed what, for the sake of this study, might be described as a moderate level of participation in the *reportatio* process, one that was limited to emendation; in the second, he was involved to the point of at least some actual composition; in the third, he seems to have had no input all.[16]

In *The Mystic Ark*, it seems that Hugh's participation was something else again, being less than the moderate level of participation described by Laurence but more than that of the apparently completely independent *reportatio* of *De contemplatione*.

2. THE OCCASIONAL LACK OF UNDERSTANDING OF THE REPORTER OF BOTH THE CONCEPT AND THE PAINTING OF *THE MYSTIC ARK*

While the evidence of this particular *reportatio* process manifests itself most clearly in a general reading of the entire body of the writing, let me point out a few of the more pronounced indications of the origins of *The Mystic Ark* as a *reportatio* without detailing every single occurrence, which are many.

Perhaps the most obvious specific evidence that *The Mystic Ark* is a *reportatio* lies in a lack of clarity and even a confusion so consistent that it is all but impossible that the text was directly written by Hugh, an author who—like Bernard of Clairvaux—never lets his eye drift from the target.[17] Sometimes these slips manifest themselves as an absence of true understanding of the fundamental logic of the structure of *The Mystic Ark*.

For example, following the description of the construction of the central cubit with which *The Mystic Ark* begins, the Ark proper is taken up (Fig. 2, no. 11). Here, the text mentions (using the present subjunctive) that the rectangle that is to become the first stage "ought" to have a length six times its width, according to the biblical dimensions, but immediately goes on to state (using the perfect indicative) that "I myself have shortened the length to around four times."[18] The purpose of this modification is to decrease the size of the Ark "because of its more suitable form": so that, rather than have an extreme oblong shape, the world with which the Ark is more or less coterminous—and which is traditionally circular—would have to be only oval, properly speaking (Fig. 7). This is a reduction that determines every other aspect of the size of the painting and that, in its willingness to alter not just divine proportions but the

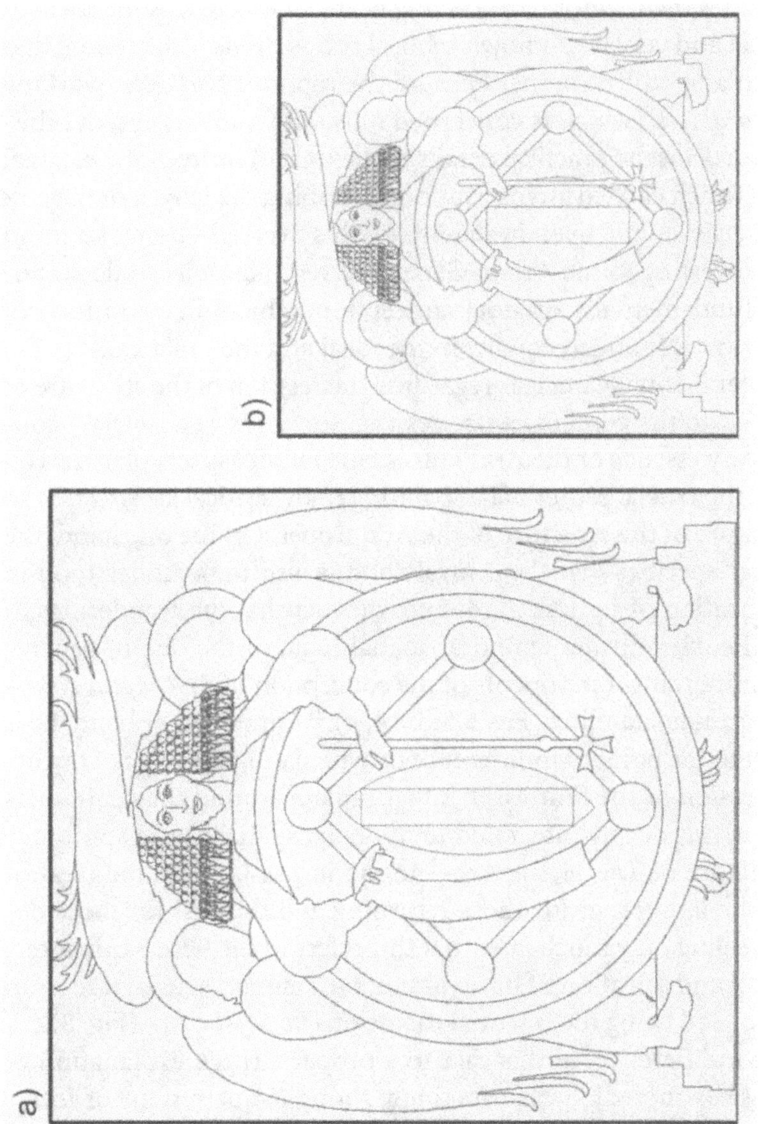

Fig. 7. *The Mystic Ark*. Proportions. (a) According to biblical proportions (Ark 300 x 50 cubits). (b) According to Hugh's revised proportions (Ark 200 x 50 cubits). Clement/Rudolph.

divine proportions of the basic structure of the painting, can come only from the authority of Hugh, not a student reporter. A few sentences further on, however, in the discussion of the construction of the second and third stages, the reporter notes (in the present indicative now and oblivious to any change), "I construct two more rectangles similarly having lengths six times their width," conceiving of the new stages as identical to the traditional and very well-known biblical proportions of six to one that had just been altered.[19] Whether because the reporter had been working from *The Moral Ark* (which is concerned only with a discussion of biblical proportions, not the practical details of the image) or from the original image itself (which carried an inscription describing the length of the Ark as 300 cubits, the length given in the Bible), this oversight betrays a mind unwittingly reverting to the Ark of Genesis rather than fully understanding Hugh's fundamentally original conception, which, like so much of Hugh's thought, is founded equally in the ideal and the practical.[20]

The reporter is equally unclear regarding the relation of the structure of *The Mystic Ark* to the content of its message, something completely contrary to the very essence of the *Ark*. This is true for all aspects of *The Mystic Ark*, from the crucial center of the painting to the critical ascents that so define the nature of the structure of the Ark proper. On the one hand, the reporter never specifies that the central cubit is also to be understood in part as the location of Jerusalem, despite the fact that the wanderings of the Chosen People and the temporal-spatial logic of the line of generation—both important components of the conception of *The Mystic Ark*—rely upon this understanding (Fig. 5, no. 14, 4).[21] On the other hand, he is vague almost to the point of indifference in articulating the logic of the order of progression of the four ascents that radiate around the central cubit—a logic that is deeply integrated temporally, spatially, and spiritually into the structure of *The Mystic Ark*—noting in passing that the Heat of the East is "the last corner for those returning and the first for those departing," revealing only much later that this refers to the necessarily interdependent fall and salvation of humankind: humankind's departure from and return to God being the essential theme of *The Mystic Ark* (Fig. 8).[22]

The same indifference, in this case to a proper written explanation of *The Mystic Ark*'s incredibly painstakingly thought-out system of interrelated logic, is the basis of the almost total lack of indication of where the only seemingly irregular (and then just slightly) set of inscriptions belongs—this set being made up of three triads rather than the four triads that is standard in the *Ark* (headed by The Married, Those Making Use of the World, and The Things That Creep)—a set whose very irregularity suggests its importance to Hugh.[23]

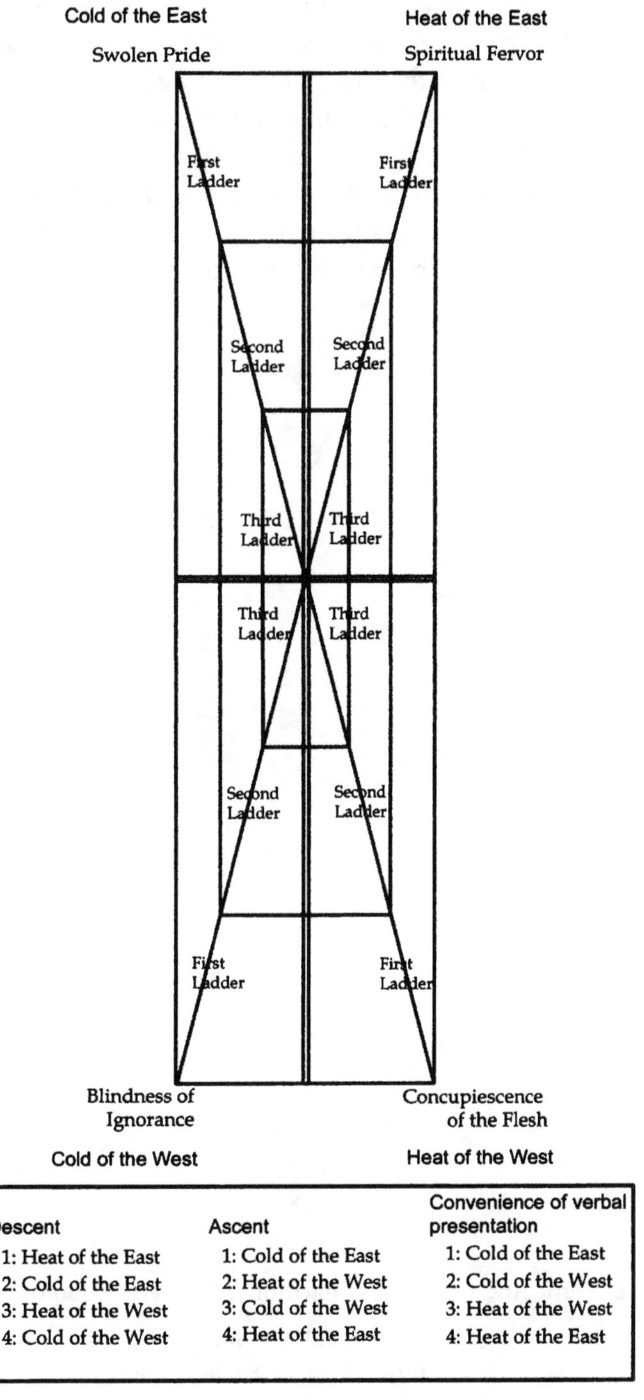

Descent	Ascent	Convenience of verbal presentation
1: Heat of the East	1: Cold of the East	1: Cold of the East
2: Cold of the East	2: Heat of the West	2: Cold of the West
3: Heat of the West	3: Cold of the West	3: Heat of the West
4: Cold of the West	4: Heat of the East	4: Heat of the East

Fig. 8. *The Mystic Ark.* The four ascents. Clement/Rudolph.

And in his presentation of the quaternary harmony that plays such a significant and delicate role in relating the basic soteriological nature of *The Mystic Ark* to the current controversy over advanced learning, the reporter hopelessly confuses the tightly interconnecting elements that correlate the time and space of the cosmos to the individual: first associating Spring with the East (the top of the painting) and then, two paragraphs later, associating Summer with the same top (Fig. 2, no. 9; Fig. 9). This error apparently came about through the reporter's consultation of a schema from a literary source for this particular component (which had

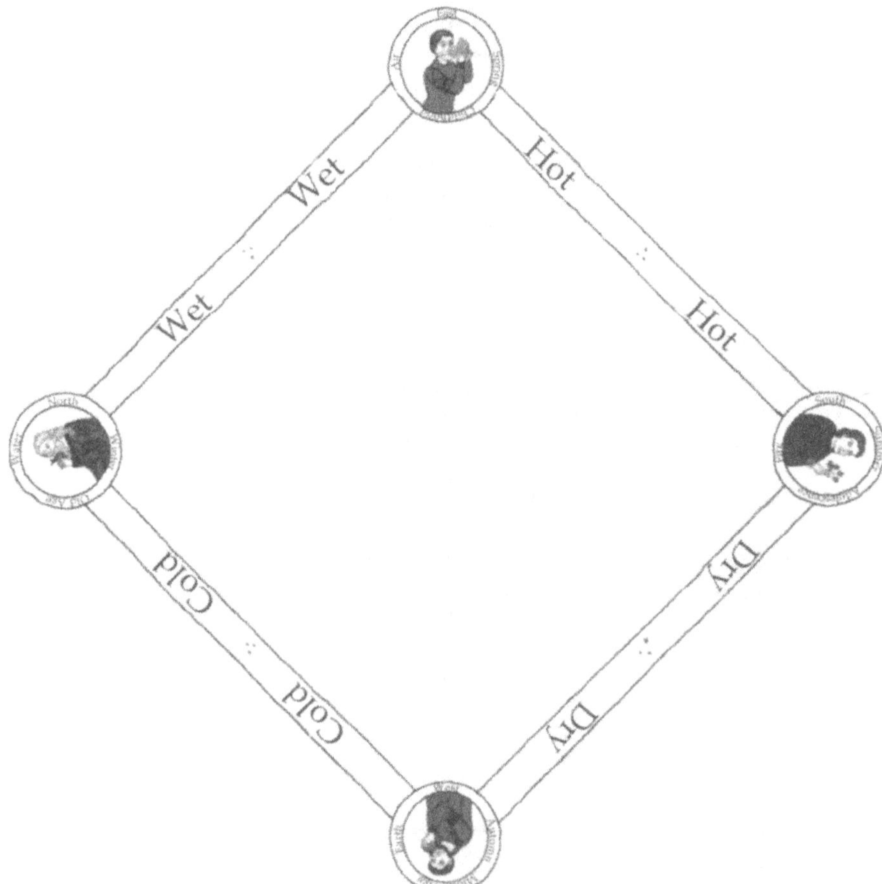

Fig. 9. *The Mystic Ark.* Quaternary harmony. Clement/Rudolph.

1: East/Childhood/Air/Spring
2: South/Adolescence/Fire/Summer
3: West/Middle age/Earth/Autumn
4: North/Old age/Water/Winter

such a strong literary tradition)—such as the schema illustrating the chapter on the four elements in Isidore of Seville's *De natura rerum*—rather than from direct observation of the painting itself as the text was written (cf. Figs. 9 and 10, for example).[24] This he would have done because of his relative unfamiliarity with this seemingly complex but actually quite simple and entirely traditional "scientific" component, and because he knew that the schema of Isidore (among other possibilities) and *The Mystic Ark* replicated the same concept. He was oblivious to the fact, whether through indifference or inexperience, that this very common schema has a variable orientation that had to be made to agree with *The Mystic Ark*'s own four cardinal directions, which are an important component of the *Ark*. Not only is such an error indicative of an individual

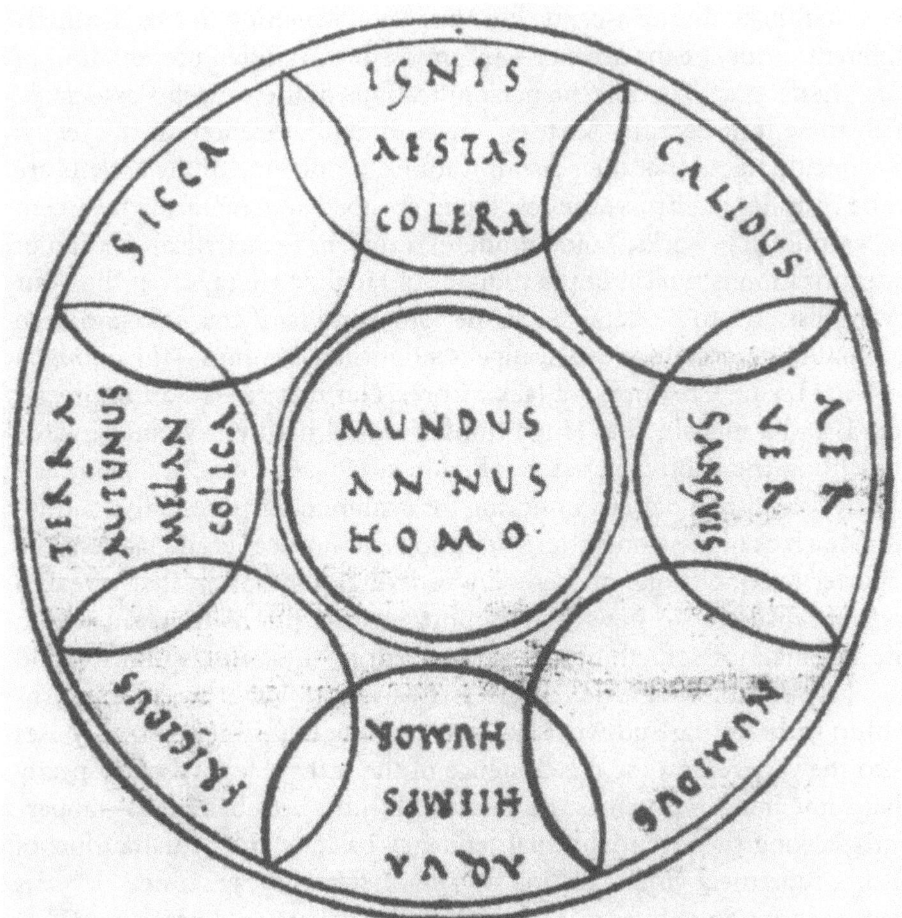

Fig. 10. Macro/microcosmic harmony. Isidore of Seville, *De Natura Rerum*. Bibliothèque nationale de France, Ms. lat. 5543:136.

who was not very advanced, but it is also suggestive of one who was, at the most basic level, not in harmony with the logic of *The Mystic Ark*. The practice itself of turning to the library to work up the details of the written text, however, is exactly that of the *reportatio* process as described by Smalley, although the particular reason for doing so here would have been unnecessary for virtually any experienced scholar—not to mention that the act was quite clumsily effected.

Distinct from this lack of connection with the logic of the structure of *The Mystic Ark*, a general carelessness of description pervades the text that is completely foreign to those writings by Hugh himself, whose clarity, precision, and organization have caused him to be described as one of the first of the scholastics. For example, in one passage, the reporter calls the all-important ascents (each ascent comprising a triad of ladders) *scalae*, while at the same time using the same word for the individual ladders that make up the ascents, but then later switching to two distinctly different terms for the ascents—an impossibly muddled presentation of *The Mystic Ark*.[25] He calls the personifications of the concepts associated with these four ascents "Virtues," even though elsewhere in the text it is explicitly stated that the personifications of only one of the ascents are to be considered virtues, the rest being grouped systematically by ascent as "emotions," "works," and "thoughts"; this more analytical method of categorization is typical of the thought of Hugh.[26] He says that the Four Evangelists are to be depicted at the four corners of the Ark, and then goes on to describe not the Evangelists but their symbols—the *animalia* or Four Living Creatures—a lack of precision that reveals an imprecise mind, and a mistake that Hugh himself would hardly have made when presenting the subject in a school context (Fig. 2, no. 12).[27] Despite a clearly established pattern of noting for symbolic purposes either a division or a lack of division of the inscriptions of the ascents and ladders, the reporter overlooks one of these, a wandering of attention that reveals a lack of sensitivity to how these important inscriptions function within the schema, not something the very author of these inscriptions would be likely to do.[28] He often neglects to indicate what are inscriptions within the painting and what are not, a failing that is at cross-purposes with the very reason for the existence of the text.[29] He forgets to specify that some imagery, such as the Twelve Months, is to be figural—apparently lacking the essential visual tendency basic to the actual author of such a supremely visual creation as *The Mystic Ark* (Fig. 2, no. 7).[30] His level of attention to history is low—something that could never be said of Hugh himself. The reporter mentions the Babylonian Captivity before the liberation from Egypt, a small point but a telling one that, in its ahistorical attitude, is contrary to the deeply historical outlook of both Hugh and *The Mystic Ark* (Fig. 5, no. 15, 14).[31] Likewise, in a passage devoted to the six ages of the history of salvation, the reporter never describes these ages as being in any way coordinated with the rest of the image, though the context of the passage suggests that they were (Fig. 11).[32] He confuses the traditional order of exegetical levels, at one point giving the sequence of history, allegory, and tropology as history, tropology, and allegory, something that in its blatant inattention to the spiritual ascent inherent in the different levels of exegetical understanding—a subject with which *The Mystic Ark* is intimately concerned—is absolutely inconceivable as coming directly from Hugh, about whom no less a personage than Bonaventure said, after identifying certain individual Fathers with the various levels of exegetical interpretation, that only he excelled at all of them.[33] Even worse from the point of view of the basic function of the text of *The Mystic Ark*, which is to provide a description for constructing the image, this misordering comes in the highly detailed account of various ladders of the ascents—a real impediment for successful completion and use of the *Ark*. And the reporter wavers in his point of reference, normally describing the painting from the point of view of looking out from the image (where the term "right" means stage right, or the left as viewed), but in more than one place describing it both from this point of view and from that of looking directly toward it (where the term "right" means the viewer's right, or stage left).[34] This inconsistency indicates the absence of a firm grasp of the importance of the essential relation of the image to the viewer. The first point of view, which conceives of the painting as the subject from which knowledge emanates, is indifferently abandoned for the second, which sees it simply as the subject of description: the point of view of the actual author, Hugh, becomes unwittingly transformed into the point of view of the mere writer, the reporter.

Hugh is a scholar who advocated the very careful use of color as a memory aid—a practice in which the slightest mistake renders the device counterproductive—and color is a very significant element in *The Mystic Ark*.[35] Yet the reporter has an extremely lax attitude toward color indeed. For example, in his discussion of the planks of the three periods, he mentions the use of color even before he takes up the logic of the planks but discusses these colors without actually specifying them; he then gives a partial interpretation of the significance of the colors, even though they still have not been specified (Fig. 11). He finally gives the colors after several pages of general discussion of the composition and significance of the planks, whose expression in the painting is strongly dependent on the use of these colors, but then immediately conceptually relates one of

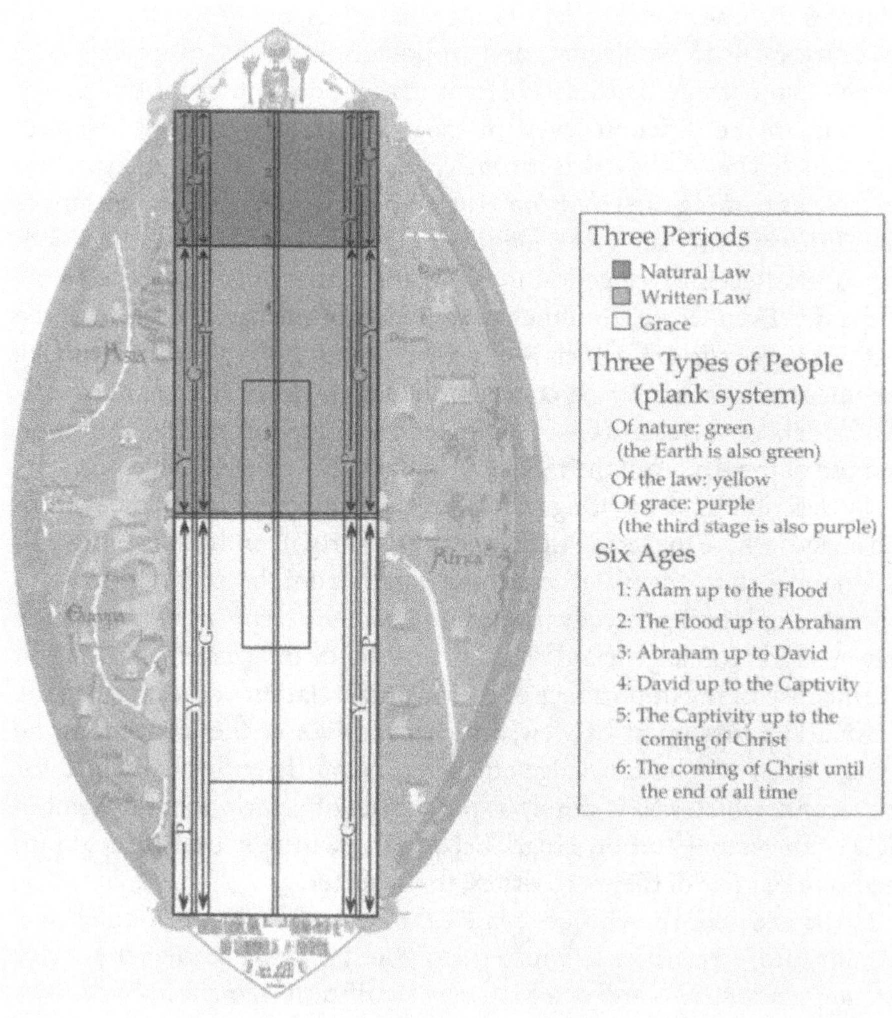

Fig. 11. *The Mystic Ark.* Time-related components of the Ark. Clement/Rudolph.

the colors (green) in the vaguest possible manner to the same color elsewhere in the schema (in the *mappa mundi*; Fig. 2, no. 10), although this component will not be mentioned for many, many pages and the use of color within it is never taken up at all.[36] Elsewhere, the reporter notes how each step on the outside of the ladders of the Cold of the East and the Cold of the West (every one of which is inscribed with the title of one of the thirty books of Scripture) is divided into three sections to indicate the book's potential for interpretation according to the three levels of exegetical thought, indicating only much later how this division is to be achieved compositionally: through the use of symbolic colors.[37]

Even more out of character is the display of a weak knowledge of the Bible. One of the distinguishing features of the line of generation is the series of "icons" of the sons of Jacob, the Patriarchs of the twelve tribes of Israel, arranged "as if a kind of senate of the City of God" (Fig. 5, no. 5). The maternity of these men, born of different women, was a very popular historical and exegetical subject in the Middle Ages. And yet the reporter confuses the mothers who were servingwomen, describing Bilhah as the servant of Leah and identifying Zilpah as the servant of Rachel, when, in fact, it was just the reverse. This is hardly the sort of mistake that a person would be likely to make who was "in knowledge of Scripture, second to none in the world," according to one twelfth-century author.[38] And yet, it is an error into which a student reporter might quite easily fall.

3. PATTERNS OF PRESENTATION WITHIN THE TEXT

The Mystic Ark would be a complex text even if it had been recorded by a very clear and disciplined individual. But it was not. Close analysis reveals faint traces of three successive, unintentionally slightly different sections of text, sections that were the result of three successive, slightly different approaches to the *reportatio* process as the work progressed. There are occasional inconsistencies within these sections, inconsistencies that are themselves sometimes significant in understanding the *reportatio* origin of *The Mystic Ark*.

The first of these unintentionally slightly different sections continues in a more or less even fashion from the beginning of *The Mystic Ark* until the theme of the four ascents is taken up, approximately half-way through the text. It is characterized by a very strong pattern of presenting first a passage of directions for the production of the Ark proper written in the first-person singular, "I," followed by a discussion of its meaning (or of how a particular aspect of the structure of the Ark is to be understood in the context of the entire construction) in the third person, with this alternation then repeated over and over again. The second section runs from the discussion of the four ascents up to the introduction of the cosmos. Here, generally speaking, the presentation changes to one of directions in the third person (as opposed to first), followed, as before, by third-person interpretations of meaning. In the third section, from the introduction of the cosmos to the end of the text, the use of first-person directions returns, generally displacing the third-person directions, except that now the first person consistently appears in the plural "we," as opposed to the earlier, more immediate singular "I." More significantly, passages of formal interpretation cease to appear, for all practical purposes.[39]

Let me characterize these sections a little further to give a better understanding of the changing *reportatio* process with which the text of *The Mystic Ark* was created. The first section begins with a very clear and detailed discussion in the first-person singular of the central cubit, followed by its thorough interpretation in the third person: this was clearly work that had been carefully gone over and, when seen in relation to the rest of the text of *The Mystic Ark*, it was clearly work that had been gone over by Hugh to one degree or another.[40] The pairing of a first-person direction passage with a third-person interpretation is a natural one here. The actual process of the production of the *Ark* proper is not part of the conceptual logic of *The Mystic Ark*, as will be discussed below, and so it would not have been part of the lectures; and so the reporter would not have had any rough notes on this aspect of the painting of *The Mystic Ark* from the lecture. This first section lays out the basic structure of the Ark and involves, at times, some fairly complex geometry.[41] To someone without any visual facility and not truly intellectually connected with the concept of the *Ark* in any profound way (as I have already shown the reporter to be) it seems that actually working up the *reportatio* from the extant painting of *The Mystic Ark* was not possible, at least in regard to the structure of *Ark*. It thus seems that Hugh personally went over the process of the basic construction with the reporter, something that should be thought of as a private lecture of sorts, not as a session of dictation with the reporter writing everything down, word for word. The use of the first-person singular here, whether simply a rhetorical device as described by Smalley or an actual vestige of this exchange, marks a presentation by Hugh that was part of the *reportatio* process but not part of the original lectures of *The Mystic Ark*. The interpretation passages that come after the direction passages generally follow the most common written form used in exegetical discussions, the third person, a form that Hugh typically uses in his own exegesis, and it would be natural to assume he used this form in the oral presentation of his lectures. The vast majority of these interpretation passages typically have a specificity that ties them to the image of the *Ark*, have no counterpart in the body of Hugh's writings, and are in all likelihood based on the reporter's original notes from the lectures. The alternation between first-person direction passages and third-person interpretation passages undoubtedly read perfectly well to the reporter, just as it does today.

The next pair of direction and interpretation passages is much the same as the first, except that it is in this direction passage that the reduction of the proportions of the Ark mentioned above is first noted and then ignored.[42] How could such a thing have come about? It is unlikely that either Hugh or the reporter forgot about this change in the few sentences that come between the two references. Rather, it seems that the vehicle was a *reportatio* process that unwittingly allowed such mistakes to slip by. It seems that, in the editing process of the no longer extant rough draft, Hugh noted (apparently orally) the reduction in proportions at the first of these two references—an alteration that could only have come from him—and that the reporter then neglected to harmonize the following text as he should have done, a text that would have agreed perfectly well before this revision in its dutiful recording of the well-known proportions of Genesis.[43] Thus, Hugh's revision was duly accepted, but Hugh himself apparently never reviewed the revised text for thoroughness, and so never caught the new error that sprang up through the careless practice of the reporter.

The same flawed process seems to account for the passage that details the six ages of the history of salvation but then neglects to specify how this subject appears in the painting (Fig. 11). Breaking the first section's pattern of a first-person direction passage followed by its interpretation in the third person, the passage on the six ages incongruously appears as a third-person narrative—neither a direction nor an interpretation—right in the middle of a long first-person direction. Easily overlooked as a meaningless inconsistency, it is precisely such hidden clues that inform us of the working process of the reporter. For the third-person passage on the six ages, unlike those passages in the first person that precede and follow it, is taken directly from Bede's *De temporum ratione*, Bede in turn having adapted it from Augustine.[44] Medieval maps and other schemata at times incorporated substantial textual passages, and there would be nothing unusual in inserting passages from Bede into the painting of *The Mystic Ark*. But the complete absence of any directions to these passages implies that they were inserted as an afterthought and perhaps from a written text rather than from the painting itself, very possibly after Hugh had pointed out that the subject had been overlooked in the mass of images and inscriptions that occupy the Ark, especially the general area of the first half of the line of generation proper. This use of the third person in a non-interpretation passage that seems not to have been part of the rough draft suggests, though it does not confirm, that the only other third-person non-interpretation passage in the first section is also an addition whose original absence may have been noticed by Hugh in a cursory review of the rough draft, this being a direction passage on the beams that become the basis of the four ascents, a passage that, this time, comes disconcertingly in the middle (again) of a very long third-person interpretation passage.[45]

Another anomaly in the first section seems to have come about in a similar way. While the written presentation of *The Mystic Ark* can be very uneven, now with a moderate amount of discussion and now less, as if dependent on the uneven lecture notes of the reporter, one subject stands out from the entire text for the great length to which it is articulated: the concept of the periods of natural law, the written law, and grace (Fig. 11). In fact, the discussion is so distinct that Sicard sees its appearance in *The Mystic Ark* as the original presentation by Hugh of a new development of his thought.[46] But for a prolific author like Hugh to publish such a developed discourse as an original presentation in a text of this genre with its otherwise minimal discussions and generally careless work would be completely inconsistent with both the evidence of Hugh's practice and the genre itself, and so more than a little unlikely. The reason for its presence in *The Mystic Ark* seems to lie elsewhere.

The subject of the three periods of the history of salvation is composed of three distinct passages. As is normal in the first section, the subject begins with a first-person direction (the first passage), which is perfectly clear, except that it refers to the colors used in distinguishing the periods without actually specifying them. These colors are given only in the third passage, which, significantly enough, is a third-person interpretation passage agreeing with the usual pattern. It is, however, a somewhat confused passage and one that strangely repeats some of the information presented in the intervening passage, the error-free second passage, which is also a third-person interpretation passage.[47] Compared with other parts of *The Mystic Ark*, this intervening second passage has an amount of explanation far greater than what the norm of the text implies is sufficient for understanding the painting, although it makes no mention of the colors whatsoever. In fact, the overall discussion of the three periods would be exactly what would be expected if it had been limited to the first and third passages alone—a standard first-person direction followed by third-person interpretation—the only problem being that they are so unclear. Why should this subject of the periods of natural law, the written law, and grace have been treated so differently from the rest of the text?

In the preface to *De sacramentis*, written shortly after *The Mystic Ark*, Hugh wrote,

> I have been compelled by the desires of certain people to write this book on the sacraments of the Christian faith. I have incorporated into it a number of pieces that I had randomly written (*dictassem*) previously because it seemed laborious, even superfluous, to recompose these same points. If it happens that my plain words have been unable to observe a semblance of the art of writing in these, I have not thought it very important since they are [all] grounded in the same truth.
>
> This, however, does concern me: that, when I had written these same pieces without sufficient attention earlier—having no intention of a future work at the time—I indiscriminately made them available for copying, having thought it was enough for these short pieces, even notes, to become known. But later, when I was incorporating them into the body of this work, reason demanded that certain things in them be changed, that certain things be added or removed. . . .[48]

From this, we learn that Hugh was willing to incorporate earlier works of his into later ones and that he had been handing out these works to others.[49] We also know that the reporter was himself willing to incorporate other writings into *The Mystic Ark*, having copied directly both from Bede and from *The Moral Ark*, as a passage in the second section shows.[50] Hugh's theory of the three periods, however, was never explicitly developed in *The Moral Ark*, and the reporter could not turn to it for the error-free intervening second passage. Given that he was clearly having trouble describing this subject, it seems that this intervening passage, which has been figuratively described by Sicard as virtually an "insertion" into the text,[51] is literally just that, though not actually an original development in the sense that he means. Rather, it seems that it is in all likelihood a vestige, partially adapted by the reporter, of one of those "short pieces or even notes" that Hugh had been accumulating, that he handed out, and that he eventually integrated into longer works—perhaps even a remnant of his lost letter to Bernard of Clairvaux, to which Bernard responded with his *De baptismo* of 1127 to 1128, apologizing for its lateness.[52] Indeed, the component of color comes not from Hugh's thought on the three periods per se but from its visual expression in the painting: there is no reference to color in the intervening second passage because the second passage's exact language came from outside the *Ark* lectures, originally having been made without reference to the painting of *The Mystic Ark*. This intervening second passage, then, is an example of the type of writing mentioned by Hugh, which was given by him to help the reporter over a rough spot, and its artless integration by the reporter brought about the awkward separation of the original reference to the color scheme from its specification so many pages later, the result of a *reportatio* process that did not place a high value on consistency.

The second of the informal, unintentional sections runs from the discussion of the four ascents up to, but not including, the cosmos.[53] No new, geometrically demanding construction is a part of this section, nor are there any difficult historical-theological concepts, as was the case in the first section, where Hugh seems to have had to coach the reporter personally and to provide clarifying written material. Though complex enough in its own right, this is a section in which reference to his own lecture notes and to the painting directly seems to have been enough for the reporter for the most part. This would account for the section's generally straightforward pattern of third-person direction passages alternating with third-person interpretation passages. Indeed, in this section—which shows no obvious signs of revision by Hugh himself—the use of the first-person singular "I" ceases to appear in any consistent fashion, and mistakes begin to proliferate, the latter apparently because Hugh was no longer closely reading the rough draft. At the same time, the use of the first-person authorial plural "we" is found from time to time, but in a generally haphazard manner that suggests no direct intervention on the part of Hugh.

Even so, the reporter still occasionally feels the need for an authority other than his own lecture notes and his own uneven ability at reading the painting, at times being compelled to turn to extant writings of Hugh. The most explicit example of this occurs in the passage on the four ways of going forth from the doorway of the central pillar. Here, in an interpretation passage, the reporter borrows directly from *The Moral Ark*, whose language,

> Quatuor modis eximus. . . . Primus modus est, quando consideramus omnem creaturam quid sit ex se. . . . Secundus modus est, quando consideramus quid sit . . . ex dono creatoris. . . . Tertius modus est, quando consideramus quomodo utatur Deus ministerio creaturarum ad implenda iudicia sua. . . . Quartus modus . . . est, quando . . . homo. . . .[54]

is copied almost word for word in *The Mystic Ark*:

> Quatuor modis eximus. Primus modus est, quando consideramus omnem creaturam quid sit ex se. Secundus modus est quando consideramus omnem creaturam quid sit ex beneficio creatoris. Tertius modus est quando consideramus quomodo utatur Deus ministerio creaturarum ad implenda iudicia sua. Quartus modus est quando . . . homo. . . .[55]

Indeed, at the end of this passage, the reporter openly refers the reader to *The Moral Ark*, to which he himself had just turned.

The third of the unintentionally different sections covers the last part of *The Mystic Ark*: the cosmos and the Majesty.[56] Extremely abbreviated in tone—as if the reporter came to realize that he had taken on a bigger job than he had initially expected or perhaps for another reason to be taken up later—this section consists almost entirely of third-person direction passages; there are no interpretation passages at all in the sense of those previously found in the text. The only passages in any way approaching an exception are a short introduction to this section and a conclusion to the whole of *The Mystic Ark*, both of which are in the first-person plural. Despite the importance of these two passages, which will be discussed soon, they are too terse to give any proof either way of having been directly written by Hugh.[57]

Nevertheless, there is significant evidence of the *reportatio* nature of *The Mystic Ark* in this section. I have already mentioned the confusion over the seasonal component of the quaternary harmony caused by careless reference to a differently oriented image from a text such as Isidore's *De natura rerum* and the impossibility of ascribing this inexcusable fumbling to Hugh. But, in its own way, equally revealing and perhaps even more striking as evidence that *The Mystic Ark* was written by a reporter—striking in its immediate, personal quality—is a passage that amounts to no less than a personal comment made by the reporter on the painting itself. One of Hugh's more original historical/theological theories was that of a developed east-west temporal-spatial progression of the focal point of human history, of the history of salvation, a theory that was rather fully articulated in *The Moral Ark*.[58] According to this theory, at the beginning of human history, what might be called the focal point of human activity was what would have appeared as the extreme east on many medieval *mappae mundi:* the Garden of Eden (Fig. 5, no. 11). The focal point shifted west soon after, according to this theory, with the great Mesopotamian empires of the Assyrians, the Chaldaeans, and the Medes. Moving further west with the civilization of Classical Greece and the empire of Alexander, and further still with the Roman Empire, it reached its ultimate westernmost extension at "the end of the earth" after the fall of Rome with the advent of the centers of power and learning of Western Christendom. This theory is described in *The Mystic Ark* in the discussion of the earth as one of the three components of the cosmos:

> A map of the world is depicted in this area [i.e., the area of an ellipse, overlaid by the Ark; cf. Fig. 5] in such a way that the top of the Ark is directed toward the east and its bottom touches the west to the effect that—*in its extraordinary arrangement*—the geographical layout of the sites extends downward in sequence with the events of time from the same beginning, and the end of the world is the same as the end of time.[59]

Far from taking this dimensional phenomenon of the history of salvation a step further as Hugh does in *The Moral Ark* by relating the length, width, and height of the Ark to the exegetical categories of history, allegory, and tropology, the reporter of *The Mystic Ark* completely ignores this aspect—though such an exegetical attitude is a constant undercurrent of *The Mystic Ark*—and explains even the basic historical theory rather poorly. Indeed, "its extraordinary arrangement" (*mirabili dispositione*) is a comment on the ingenuity of the painting's ability to express Hugh's theory, not on the theory itself. It is the passive reaction of an observer to the painting, not the active exposition by an experienced intellectual of one of his own original theories. It is as if the intellectually unaccomplished reporter were standing back, looking at the painting, and felt that it was enough to praise the subject at hand; it is inconceivable that such a statement should have been made by Hugh himself. That this was done through direct visual observation is confirmed by the extremely specific and entirely unnecessary directions regarding the depiction of the Winds and the arrangement of the figures of the Zodiac and Months, something that could only be site-specific (Fig. 2, no. 8, 6, 7).[60]

In the end, this last section shows no evidence of any close oversight by Hugh, whether in the form of personal revision, personal instruction, or the lending of unpublished material.

And so it seems that these three unintentionally slightly different sections of text were the result of three successive, slightly different approaches to the *reportatio* process as the work of the reporter progressed. The first section—whose component of the geometric structure of the Ark was crucial to the painting of *The Mystic Ark*, but which by its very nature had not been part of the original lecture series and so for which the reporter could have taken no notes—shows evidence that much of it was based on a private talk given by Hugh to the reporter to explain this structure. There is also evidence that Hugh gave the reporter some of his own, more extensive notes on at least one other subject that appeared in this section, and that the reporter readily resorted to related outside literary sources to fill out his text. In the second section, which contains no demanding geometric constructions or difficult concepts for which the reporter might have had to turn to Hugh, the reporter seems to have depended more on direct reference to the painting, on his own lecture notes, and on continued reference to outside texts, in this case Hugh's *The Moral Ark*. The reporter continued to make direct visual reference to the painting and to refer to outside written sources in the third section, although this section is distinguished by the virtually complete absence of interpretation passages, perhaps because the magnitude of the task had begun to make itself felt or perhaps for another reason, which I will take up further on.

4. "TECHNICAL TERMS"

Finally, the objection has been made by another scholar, Michael Evans, that "Hugh's diction throughout is odd," and that words such as *planities, cingulus, zona, limbus*, and *cornu* are not "the idiom of the practicing artist."[61] No, they are not the idiom of the practicing artist. Hugh was not a practicing artist, and, so it seems, far less was the reporter; and so there is no reason at all to expect the language of the *reportatio* of *The Mystic Ark* to be that of a practicing artist. What Hugh was, was a master of the schools. And what the reporter was, was a practicing student. As such, *The Mystic Ark* understandably, if awkwardly at times, employs the language of the schools that was so familiar to them both.

Thus, when the first of the unintentionally different sections of *The Mystic Ark* mentioned above—the one that seems to have been the result of a private lecture of sorts given by Hugh on the geometric structure of the Ark for the benefit of the reporter—opens with, "First, I find the center point on the surface (*planitie*) where I wish to depict the Ark . . .," the word *planities* is used by the reporter either because that was how Hugh described the geometric process of finding the center point during the private lecture or because that was how the reporter himself conceived the clearest explanation of the geometric process described to him by Hugh: *planities* being a common geometrical term used both in Hugh's *Practica geometriae* and, presumably, in any course on geometry the reporter may have taken from Master Hugh at Saint Victor.[62] Indeed, the term is defined in the geometric sense of "surface" in the widely read school text *Commentary on the Dream of Scipio* by Macrobius (Macrobius was referred to repeatedly in Hugh's *Practica geometriae*), this usage also being found in Vitruvius, who is referred to by Hugh in his *Didascalicon*, the latter being a guide to study for students at Saint Victor.[63]

Cingulus and *zona*—which the same author who found the use of *planities* "odd" feels "derive as a group from the vocabulary of the gentleman's outfitter"—likewise either come or could come right out of the *Commentary on the Dream of Scipio*.[64] In the same way that Macrobius begins his discussion of the different climatic divisions of the world employing the word *cingulus* (which I translate as "belt") and later switches to *zona* ("band"), using both words interchangeably, the reporter follows the same pattern in his discussion of the great bands that extend across the entire length and breadth of the Ark, which is itself virtually coterminous with the earth on all four sides, conceiving of these bands as essentially cosmic in scope (reflecting the thought of Hugh), however awkward the language may seem to a modern reader.[65] And just as the *zonae* of Macrobius and other classical writers (such as Virgil, Ovid, and Pliny) distinguish the different climatic zones of the world—the frigid, temperate, and torrid—the *zonae* of *The Mystic Ark* distinguish the Heat of the East from the Cold of the East, the Heat of the West from the Cold of the West, and so on.[66] A glance at a Macrobian zonal map makes very plain how the colored horizontal and diagonal bands of a map like this could have been transposed in the mind of the reporter (or Hugh) to the colored horizontal and vertical bands of *The Mystic Ark* (Fig. 12).[67]

Limbus, likewise, is a word that Honorius Augustodunensis does not hesitate to use in his *Imago Mundi*—another text addressed to school culture—to describe the "border" or limits of the world in much the same way that the reporter uses it to describe the border of the central cubit (Fig. 13).[68]

As to the use of *cornu* to mean "corner" (seven occurrences), it is enough to say that although *cornu* is a perfectly acceptable word for corner, the more common term for this meaning in *The Mystic Ark* is *angulus* (sixteen occurrences), the same term employed by Hugh in *The Moral Ark*, where the word *cornu* is never used.[69] Thus, in that work that is unequivocally written by Hugh himself, *The Moral Ark*, the terminology is "standard." It is only in the *reportatio* that the language becomes perhaps a bit more arcane, whether as a demonstration of newly acquired Latin skills on the part of the reporter or because of the common usage of *cornu* in reference to the corners of an altar—the most common use of the word for a young ecclesiastic—which in plan shares the same shape as the Ark.[70]

So while it is impossible to say whether the particular choices of most of these "technical terms" came from Hugh or from the reporter, the word *planities* seems to have come from the *reportatio* process, and *planities, cingulus, zona*, and *limbus* are all from the language of the schools: not the language of a "practicing artist," but of the world from which Hugh and the reporter came, from which the painting and text of *The Mystic Ark* came, and in which *The Mystic Ark* functioned.

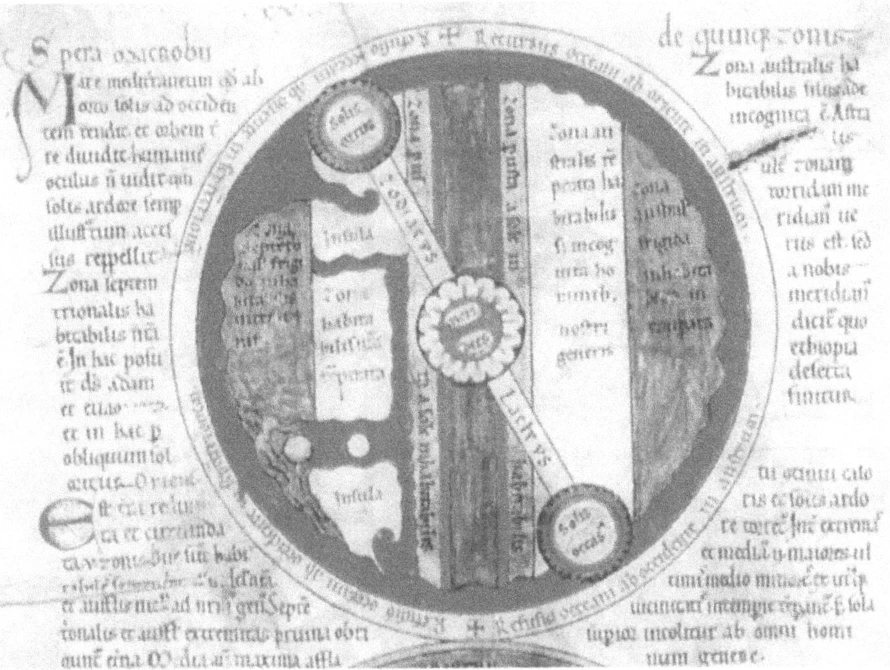

Fig. 12. *Sphera Macrobii*. Lambert of Saint-Omer, *Liber Floridus*. Herzog August Bibliothek Wolfenbüttel, Ms. 1 Gud. lat. fol. 16v.

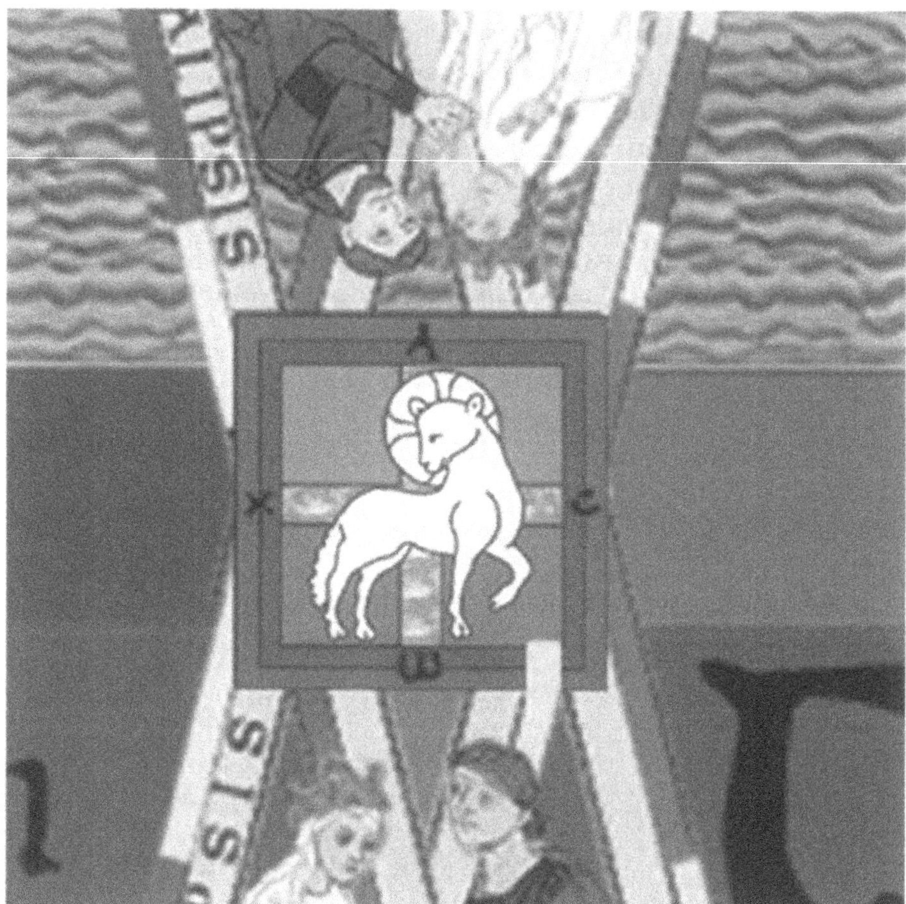

Fig. 13. *The Mystic Ark.* The central cubit. Clement/Rudolph.

Chapter Two

THE SUPPOSITION OF A CONTINUING CHANGE IN *THE MYSTIC ARK*

After the realization that the text of *The Mystic Ark* is a *reportatio*, perhaps the greatest difficulty in coming to terms with its nature and function lies in understanding the relation between it, the painting of *The Mystic Ark*, and the treatise of *The Moral Ark*—a relationship that is quite simple and straightforward. A failure to recognize the simplicity of this relationship, accompanied by strained explanations for supposed complexities, constitutes Sicard's second basic error of interpretation.

The question of whether the image referred to in *The Moral Ark* is the same as that described in *The Mystic Ark* is not really at issue.[71] What is at issue, at least to Sicard, are the seeming inconsistencies between *The Moral Ark* and the text of *The Mystic Ark*, inconsistencies that suggest to him that Hugh's conception of *The Mystic Ark* changed throughout the course of his lectures. According to Sicard, the lost original image of the lectures should be thought of as having presented only the initial stage in this change, a stage represented by the text of *The Moral Ark*. He believes that the text of *The Mystic Ark*, on the other hand, should be understood as presenting a supposed later stage that came about after the *Ark* lectures and their expression in *The Moral Ark*, a stage that represents a much fuller conception of the *Ark*. Furthermore, having identified two recensions of the manuscript tradition, Sicard believes that the first recension represents the initial expression of this fuller conception; while the revisions of the second recension indicate yet more changes by Hugh himself as well as a hopelessly failed attempt at a simplification of the careless text of the first recension. None of these suppositions, however, seems to be the case.

1. THE SUPPOSITION OF A CONTINUING CHANGE FROM THE ORIGINAL PAINTING OF *THE MYSTIC ARK* TO THE *REPORTATIO* OF *THE MYSTIC ARK*

The first supposition, that there had been a continuing change from the original painting of *The Mystic Ark* to the *reportatio* of *The Mystic Ark*, is related to the subject of the relative chronology of the *Ark* lectures and texts. As I mentioned earlier, as a result both of a reference in *The Mystic Ark* to *The Moral Ark* as already written and of the repeated indication in *The Moral Ark* that the painting of *The Mystic Ark* was already extant, the traditional view has been that *The Moral Ark* was written first, with the text of *The Mystic Ark* following shortly after, so that it might provide a written description of the image referred to in *The Moral Ark*.

This has been further elaborated by Damien van den Eynde, who has worked out basic relative and absolute chronologies of the works of Hugh.[72] Van den Eynde uses Hugh's *Sententie de divinitate* as the fixed point around which he establishes his relative chronology of the *Ark* texts, seeing *The Moral Ark* as having been written shortly before the *Sententie* and *The Mystic Ark* as shortly after. Keeping the intricacies of his argument to a minimum, let me say that van den Eynde's overall structure of a number of groupings of the complete body of Hugh's works appears sound, though the exact relative order within the particular group in which *The Mystic Ark* is placed seems to need further work.

For example, he argues that *The Moral Ark* precedes the *Sententie* because the discussion of the works of creation and of restoration in *The Moral Ark* is "rambling" and "scattered," while the *Sententie* presents the same subject more systematically.[73] What van den Eynde fails to take into consideration is that *The Moral Ark* is an example of a literary genre that attempts to evoke a *collatio* or intellectual/spiritual discussion among highly educated participants. As such, it is experiential in feeling and privileges a more or less conversational presentation of its immediate topic—the instability of the human heart and the restoration of the soul to its creator—over any more focused or systematic theological presentation, though it is fundamentally informed by theology and systematic modes of thought. The *Sententie*, on the other hand, is a *reportatio* of an early form of Hugh's greatest systematic theology, the *De sacramentis*. As such, a systematized basic format is nothing less than mandatory. The discussions of the works of creation and of restoration in the two writings are equally true to their own genres.

In a somewhat similar vein, van den Eynde's discussion of the relation between the *Sententie* and *The Mystic Ark* is based on the seeming theological development of the concept of the periods of natural law, the written law, and grace, mentioned above.[74] In this, it suffers from a lack of awareness that *The Mystic Ark* is a *reportatio* (i.e., it was not written by Hugh personally) and that the passage on the three periods in *The Mystic Ark* gives every appearance of having been based on a previously written but unpublished "short piece" or "note" given to the reporter by Hugh.

As to absolute chronology, van den Eynde establishes the date of Hugh's *Sententie de divinitate* as 1127 or a little later. He thus sees *The Moral Ark* as having been written shortly before 1127 and *The Mystic Ark* shortly after, the latter probably in 1128 or 1129.[75]

Sicard essentially subscribes to van den Eynde's chronologies, hypothesizing that Hugh's original lectures on *The Mystic Ark* were held sometime around 1125 to 1126.[76] He suggests that sometime later, around 1126 to 1127, Hugh put the material of these lectures down in writing in the form of *The Moral Ark*. Following van den Eynde, Sicard accepts 1128 or 1129 for the date of the text of *The Mystic Ark*. His argument that the conception of *The Mystic Ark* changed over the course of time focuses primarily on two major elements of the *Ark*: the three periods and the cosmos (particularly the seasonal component of the quaternary harmony).

More specifically, Sicard feels that the absolutely fundamental element of the periods of natural law, the written law, and grace was not present in the original image because it was not fully discussed in *The Moral Ark* (Fig. 11). At the same time, since the text of *The Mystic Ark* does have a full statement on the three periods of the history of salvation, he thinks that this subject was conceptually developed by Hugh only after the original lectures were held and *The Moral Ark* was written.[77] But the statement on the three periods in *The Mystic Ark* seems to be, as I have argued, an insertion by the reporter, and so would have been written sometime before the *reportatio* of *The Mystic Ark*.[78] And the fact is, whether there is a full discussion in *The Moral Ark* or not, the three periods are referred to in that treatise in such a way as to make it plain that the subject was present in an integral way in the original painting, even though there was no compelling reason for Hugh to take it up in *The Moral Ark* itself, a writing whose aims are much narrower than those of *The Mystic Ark*. For example, in *The Moral Ark*, Hugh writes about the Ark:

> The length of three hundred cubits indicates the present age, which extends through three periods: the period of natural law, the period of written law, and the period of grace.[79]

Given that he has just introduced the painting into his discussion at this point and is taking up the meaning of the length of the Ark—which is "the present age," historical time, through which the Church, which began at creation, advances toward the end of time—there would seem to be no other explanation for this reference to the three periods in the text, except that it is directly related to the presence of these periods in the image, regardless of how much or how little attention to them was useful to Hugh in the specific theme of *The Moral Ark*, which is the instability of the human heart and the restoration of the soul to its creator and not the history of salvation. Indeed, Hugh goes on in the same passage to say that

> . . . the holy Church, which began with the beginning of the world, received redemption through the immolation of the spotless Lamb in the period of grace . . . the Church, which was from the beginning of time, was redeemed at the end of an age.[80]

This is an explicit reference to the same progression depicted in *The Mystic Ark* from creation to the period of natural law, to the period of written law, and so to the Lamb of God in the central cubit, which marks the beginning of the period of grace.

Further on in *The Moral Ark*, Hugh again explicitly mentions the horizontal progression of "the natural law," "the written law," and "the period of grace," after which there is a discussion of the same triad in relation to the three successive vertical stages of the Ark (Fig. 4). *The Mystic Ark*, a two-dimensional painting, is meant to be understood three-dimensionally,[81] with the (horizontal) length of the Ark being understood as the macrocosmic temporal progression of humankind through a series of temporal periods until its communal return to its creator at the end of time, and the (vertical) height being seen as the microcosmic spiritual ascent of the individual soul through a series of spiritual states in its own particular spiritual return to its creator.[82] That Hugh is referring in *The Moral Ark* to the same, complete construct found in the image of *The Mystic Ark* is quite clear from his specific citation of this triad as "*Natura,*" "*Lex scripta,*" and "*Gratia*"—that is, as spiritual states rather than as temporal periods—these three terms being all but identical with the inscriptions from the painting of *The Mystic Ark*.[83]

Aside from this, there are a number of references in *The Moral Ark* to other components of *The Mystic Ark* that are integrally related to the three periods and that, as a whole, can only have been incorporated into the image as part of a system that included the three periods—something that necessarily was in place at the time of the writing of *The Moral Ark*. For example, Paradise, associated with Adam and so with natural law, however complex the image of Paradise is in the *Ark*, is discussed. The flight of the Chosen People from Egypt and their exile to Babylon are repeatedly referred to; Egypt and Babylon relate almost exclusively in *The Mystic Ark* to the periods of natural law and written law, respectively. The Twelve Tribes (in the form of the Twelve Patriarchs) are mentioned, these pertaining to the transition from the period of natural law to that of the written law in this particular context.[84] There is even a discussion of Hugh's east-west temporal-spatial progression of the focal point of human history, a subject that, in this context, can only have been indicated through the component of the three periods in conjunction with a *mappa mundi*. And there are a number of other images and inscriptions related to the three periods as well.[85] There is thus no doubt but that the idea of the three periods was integrated into the image referred to in *The Moral Ark* both horizontally and vertically, and in the most fundamental way, just as the text of *The Mystic Ark* has it.

The situation is the same with the cosmos, the components of which are presented in the text of *The Mystic Ark* under the traditional groupings of earth, air, and ether (Fig. 4). Sicard thinks the cosmos was not present in the original painting of *The Mystic Ark* because neither it nor its individual components are discussed in any significant way in *The Moral Ark*.[86] He thinks that the section that describes the cosmos in the text of *The Mystic Ark* is simply "optional," that the components of the cosmos "do not constitute in the eyes of Hugh an essential part of his teaching, and that he did not attach any major importance to them." This he says despite the fact that he himself cannot help but conclude that the cosmic components "not only complete the image in a harmonious fashion but the doctrinal progress that their introduction achieves is a progress toward a more complete overall vision."[87] But the vision was always there, and it was always complete; indeed, the very nature of Hugh's theory of the works of creation and of restoration is fundamentally based on such a necessarily complete vision. And, in fact, Hugh refers to "the structure of the cosmos" again and again in *The Moral Ark*, now calling it the *universitatis corpus*, now the *mundi machina*, now the *machina universitatis*—all meaning the same thing (*mundus* means both "cosmos" and "world" in Latin)—just as he calls it the *machina universitatis* in *The Mystic Ark* (through the reporter), and the *universitatis machina* in both *De tribus diebus* and *De sacramentis*.[88] He thus does refer to the general component of the cosmos in *The Moral Ark*, even though he rarely refers to its constituent parts. But if this is the case, it is not because they are not an integral part of the painting of *The Mystic Ark*, but because they are not an integral part of the specific theme of *The Moral Ark*, a point that will soon be taken up.

Still, references to these individual cosmic components are virtually constant in *The Moral Ark*. For example, regarding the zone of the earth, in his discussion of the length of the Ark—the Ark being directly imposed upon the world in the painting of *The Mystic Ark*—Hugh speaks of one's thoughts roaming from the beginning of the world to its end, something that in the context of the painting of the *Ark* would suggest that the world, in the form of a *mappa mundi*, was present at this point.[89] He refers to the Ark of the Church, a theme of Hugh's that, by definition, necessarily must reach from the beginning of the world (the *mappa mundi*) to the end.[90] He tells how all of the nations come from the four corners of the Ark as from the four corners of the earth, which they visually appear to do in the painting of *The Mystic Ark* (the sixty men and sixty women of the four ascents) and which, it is no great leap of logic to assume, they did in the painting that existed at the time of the writing of *The Moral Ark*.[91] In a discussion of the soul's ascent to God, he employs an "*exemplum*" with the world at the bottom, God at the top, and the soul in between, precisely the vertical configuration of the painting of *The Mystic Ark* and hardly a coincidence.[92] His theory of the east-west progression of the focal point of human history, in which he refers to a number of specific sites, is by definition based upon the spatial sequence of the *mappa mundi*—again, something whose absence in the original painting would be very odd, following the logic of Sicard's argument, given the presence of this theory in *The Moral Ark*.[93] And he refers to the sequence of the works of restoration from the beginning of the world to its end, something that could be conveyed in the visual context of *The Mystic Ark* only by an image of the world.[94]

The part of the cosmos that Sicard focuses on most is the seasonal component of the quaternary harmony, in the zone of the air (Fig. 2, no. 9; Fig. 9). He believes that the quaternary harmony was not present in the original painting because the confusion over the coordination of its seasonal component, as recorded in the text of *The Mystic Ark* and discussed above, would have been out of agreement with the orientation of the rest of the image.[95] However, as I have shown, not only is the text of *The Mystic Ark* a *reportatio* (and so this passage was not written by Hugh himself), but the confusion was a simple mistake introduced by the reporter as a result of working up his text from a literary source rather than from direct observation of the painting itself; there is no evidence whatsoever that this fairly straightforward component was incorrectly oriented in the original painting. And, as with the elements of the three periods and the Earth, the seasonal component of the quaternary harmony is clearly referred to in *The Moral Ark*, in fact, in the same passage mentioned earlier on the four ways of going forth that was copied by the reporter directly from *The Moral Ark* into *The Mystic Ark*.[96] In *The Moral*

Ark, the works of creation and of restoration constitute the basis of Hugh's presentation of the soul's restoration to its creator. Following Hugh's logic, there are two main ways of showing the works of creation: through the six days of creation or through the four elements.[97] In the passage just mentioned, Hugh employs the four elements in his discussion of the works of creation, since they serve his rhetorical purposes better than would the six days and, in the process, refers to the four seasons as well, both the four elements and the four seasons constituting important components of the quaternary harmony.

Furthermore, toward the end of *The Moral Ark*—in a brief synopsis that is more an overview of *The Mystic Ark* than it is a summary of *The Moral Ark*, properly speaking—Hugh says about *The Mystic Ark*, in language reminiscent of Chalcidius and others,

> What might be called the structure of the cosmos is portrayed there, and the harmony of its individual components explained.[98]

The "structure of the cosmos," the *universitatis corpus*, as the evidence of contemporary visual culture tells us, is the same structure that is described in such detail in *The Mystic Ark* as the *machina universitatis* and whose core—the quaternary harmony—includes a harmony of the elements and seasons (cf. Byrhtferth's Diagram, Fig. 14).[99] The evidence indicates, therefore, that the quaternary harmony, and so the zone of the air, was very much present in the original painting of *The Mystic Ark*, even if it was not a focus of attention in *The Moral Ark*.

As to the zone of the ether—which, along with that of the air, Sicard sees as now oval, now circular[100]—the most pervasive references to its components are those associated with the figure of Christ based on the vision of Isaiah (Isaiah 6:1–3) with which the description of the painting in *The Moral Ark* opens, and whose presence in the original painting Sicard admits (Fig. 4).[101] Here it is said that "the whole earth is filled with his majesty" (based on Isaiah 6:3), "majesty" being the term used to describe the figure of Christ in *The Mystic Ark*—and presumably in the lectures as well—as opposed to the word "glory," found in Isaiah.[102] The passage goes on to say how this figure fills "heaven and earth" (Jeremiah 23:24); how "the heaven is [his] throne, the earth [his] footstool" (Isaiah 66:1); and how "the cycle of time and the revolution of ages . . . return upon themselves"; and so on. One of the most striking things about Hugh's interpretation of the vision of Isaiah is that the wings of the seraphim covering the face and the feet of the Lord represent the eternity of God, which extends before time and after time, as it were.[103] Given that the passage from Isaiah *per se* does not immediately lend itself to this

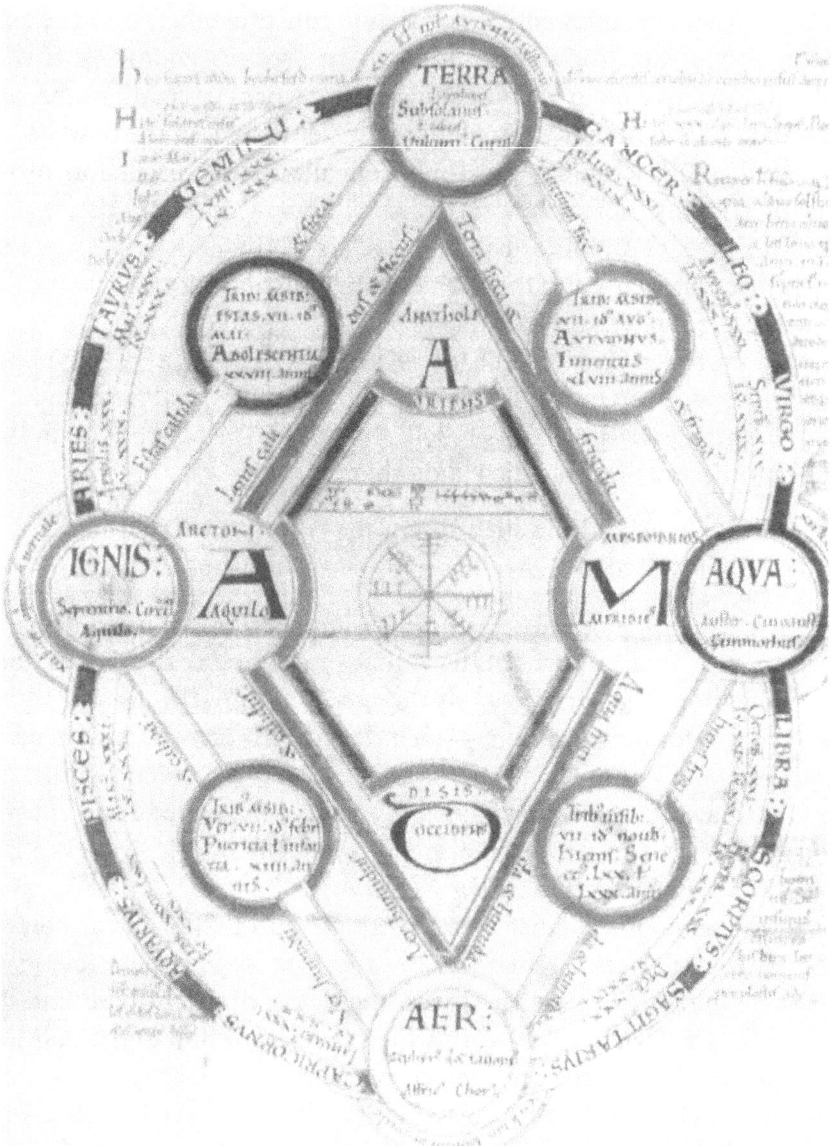

Fig. 14. Macro/microcosm (Byrhtferth's Diagram). The President and Scholars of Saint John Baptist College in the University of Oxford, Ms. 17:7v.

interpretation, and the painting of *The Mystic Ark* illustrates it beautifully—with the Lord's head and feet extending beyond the cycles of the Zodiac and Months at the top and the bottom, with all of "heaven and earth" and created time in between—it would be a strained argument that insists that the cosmos was not present in the original painting because there was not more discussion about it in *The Moral Ark*. Indeed, iconographically, the image of the Lord embracing some central object is one that is seen many times in connection with the world or the cosmos (e.g., Fig. 15), but never, to my knowledge, with the Ark alone.[104] Sicard would like to think that nothing in the section on the cosmos was in the original painting except the image of the Lord; but this is precisely why the image of the Lord was recorded in *The Mystic Ark* in the section on

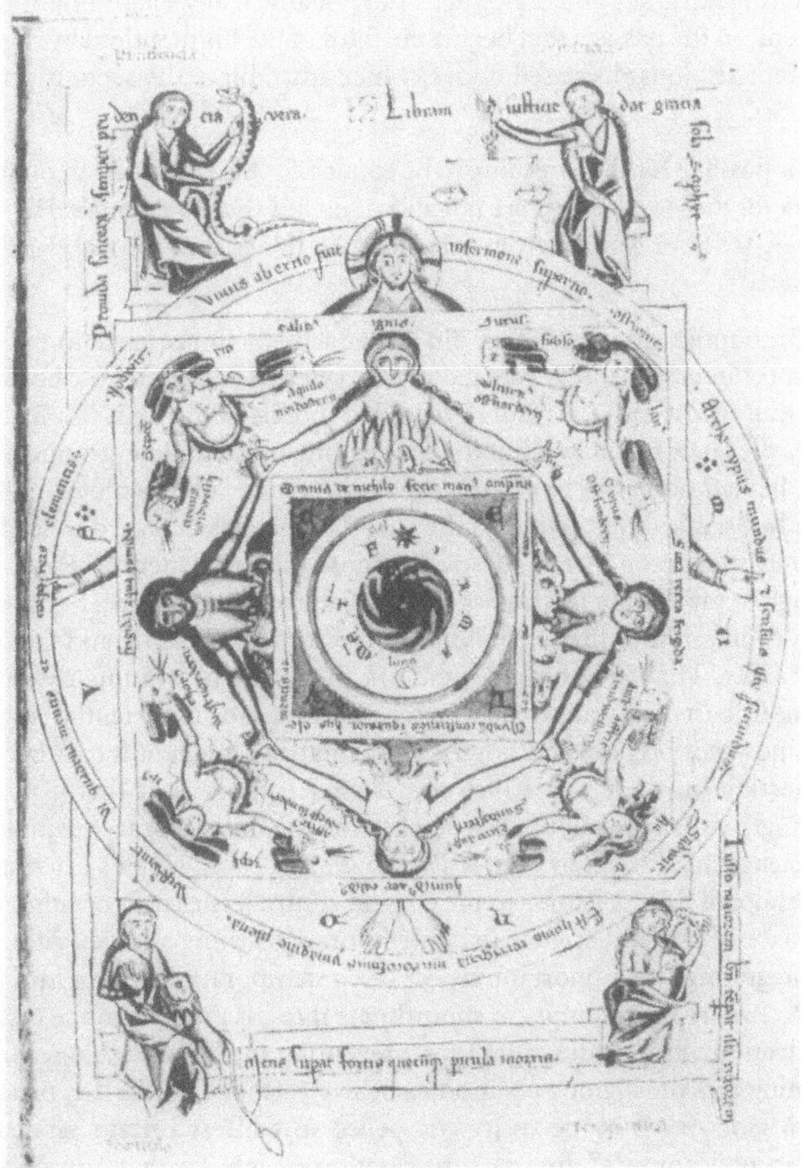

Fig. 15. Macro/microcosm. Munich, Bayerische Staatsbibliothek, Ms. CLM 2655:105.

the cosmos and not elsewhere, because it is inseparably related to the cosmos both conceptually and iconographically.

Sicard's view about the cosmic components of *The Mystic Ark* is, however, more than just a misunderstanding of the state of the original painting; it is nothing less than a misunderstanding of the polemical nature of *The Mystic Ark*. He seeks support for his view that the cosmic components are simply "optional," that they are not "an essential part of [Hugh's] teaching," and that Hugh "did not attach any major importance to them" in the passage that begins the third of the unintentionally slightly different sections discussed above, which introduces the section on the cosmos:

> It is possible for the foregoing to be enough for the construction of the Ark for those who either are not able or do not wish to do more. However, we have further given certain other things that we will briefly relate.[105]

Far from indicating that Hugh did not attach any importance to the section on the cosmos, this passage marks where *The Mystic Ark* becomes politically most delicate—not in regard to those whom Hugh would challenge, the "new theology," but to those whom, in his middle-ground position, he had no desire to offend, the conservative "old theology." I have already discussed the "old" and the "new" theologies in regard to some of the issues taken up in *The Mystic Ark* more fully elsewhere.[106] Here, it is enough to say that, in this passage, Hugh—through the reporter—is making a concession to the sensibilities of traditional monastic and collegial spirituality. The part of *The Mystic Ark* that came before this passage is primarily based on traditional exegesis and monastic experiential spirituality, however original and however systematized much of it may be. But the section on the cosmos that comes after is, at least at first glance, a strikingly visually pronounced presentation of contemporary cosmological science that forcefully relates *The Mystic Ark*—and Hugh's teaching at the school of Saint Victor—to the current controversies over creation and the place of physical science in contemporary learning and education.[107] In integrating this important aspect of contemporary learning into *The Mystic Ark*, Hugh attempts to subordinate it to his theories of the history of salvation while at the same time preventing the "new theology" from claiming this prestigious position exclusively as its own. In this process, *The Mystic Ark* is by necessity compelled to address certain aspects of "pagan philosophy's" approach to creation. Hugh—with a fair amount of political sensitivity—recognizes that certain elements of the "old theology" may be uncomfortable with the cosmic component of *The Mystic*

Ark and reluctant to reproduce it for formal discussion and education within the monastery, even though it is absolutely central to the *Ark* lectures. The section on the cosmos, thus, is no simple "option."

But there is more to it than this. As important as the individual references to cosmic components in understanding what was or was not in the original painting of *The Mystic Ark* is Hugh's own account of how the writing of *The Moral Ark* came about. Unlike the *reportatio* of *The Mystic Ark*, *The Moral Ark* opens with a fairly clear and rather evocative description of its reason for being, stemming from the original lectures at Saint Victor, concluding:

> Now, because I know that, in the discussion, certain points in particular pleased the brethren, I especially wanted to commit them to writing—not so much because I thought they were worth recording but because I knew that some of them were previously unheard of in this context and were, so to speak, all the better received because of it.[108]

In the introductory material of *The Moral Ark*, Hugh states that there are four Arks: the Ark of Noah, the Ark of the Church, the Ark of Wisdom, and the Ark of Mother Grace.[109] These four Arks were the subject of the lecture series of *The Mystic Ark*. The "certain points" that in particular pleased the brethren were Hugh's lectures (or at least part of them) on *The Moral Ark* or Ark of Wisdom: only one of the four Arks, but considered by Hugh and the brethren to be the most original part of the extended lectures that "untied the knot of each question" on the instability of the human heart.[110] Even so, Hugh does not feel that this "most original part" is best understood independently of the broader concept of *The Mystic Ark*. Thus, after discussing the cause of the instability of the human heart (love of the world) and its remedy (the building of an ark in one's soul in which God may dwell), he provides an overview of the more extensive subject of *The Mystic Ark* in general before turning his full attention to the Ark of Wisdom in particular.[111] Hugh himself gives the reason for this when he says,

> Because this ark signifies the Church and the Church is the body of Christ, in order to make the exemplar clearer to you, I have depicted the entire person of Christ—that is, the head with the members—in visible form so that, when you have seen the whole [exemplar], you should be able to understand more easily what is to be said afterwards concerning the parts.[112]

Hugh feels that "the parts"—of which *The Moral Ark* is one part only—are easier to understand after one has "seen" the whole, which he specifies as the painting of *The Mystic Ark*, calling it an exemplar (*exemplar*), the same term that is used to describe the image in the concluding passage of the text of *The Mystic Ark*.[113] Therefore, although he puts the Ark of Wisdom (the theme of *The Moral Ark*) in the context of the totality of the four Arks (*The Mystic Ark*), his subject is not the more complete view of *The Mystic Ark* that runs from the macrocosmic Ark of the Church to the microcosmic Ark of Mother Grace. And so he is not concerned in *The Moral Ark* with fully discussing those components of *The Mystic Ark* that primarily pertain to one of the other three Arks, for example, the Ark of the Church with its three periods, *mappa mundi*, quaternary harmony, or any of the other components of the *machina universitatis*. Sicard is thus wrong to expect to see in each work of Hugh's (in the manner of van den Eynde[114]) a complete statement revealing the breadth and depth of his theological development at the moment of writing, ignoring the fact that Hugh, like other authors, might now choose to take up one subject, now another. There is no reason at all why *The Moral Ark*, an explicitly circumscribed selection of the *Ark* lectures, needs to have a full presentation of the complete range of subjects of *The Mystic Ark* for those subjects to have been in the original painting of *The Mystic Ark* or in the original lectures. And there is no evidence of any continuing change of the type described by Sicard from the original painting of *The Mystic Ark* to the *reportatio* of *The Mystic Ark*.

2. THE SUPPOSITION OF A CONTINUING CHANGE FROM THE FIRST RECENSION OF *THE MYSTIC ARK* TO THE SECOND RECENSION

Sicard has identified two recensions of *The Mystic Ark*. Having never considered anything but a direct authorship by Hugh himself of *The Mystic Ark* and having misinterpreted the differences between *The Moral Ark* and *The Mystic Ark* as a continuing change, Sicard understandably—although wrongly—continues this same approach in coming to terms with the differences between the two recensions.

One recension is slightly longer than the other and received the more limited dissemination of the two.[115] The other, the slightly shorter recension, shows signs of being the result of an editing of the longer one and enjoyed the wider dissemination. Primarily for these reasons, Sicard feels that the slightly longer recension is the earlier of the two, and in this he seems to be correct.

The second recension's emendations, however, are problematic. While it is clear that the reason for revision was a half-hearted attempt to clarify the careless text of the first recension, the editor of the second recension shows even less understanding of *The Mystic Ark* than the reporter of the first. Nevertheless, Sicard believes that the second recension was also by Hugh himself, that it was done around 1135, and that some of the relatively minor edits are evidence of a continuing change in the conception of *The Mystic Ark* from the first recension to the second.[116] But, having decided that both recensions are by Hugh himself, Sicard only magnifies the problem inherent in the second recension: since the second recension was made to clarify the first but in fact really does not accomplish this, as Sicard himself points out, one is left with the conclusion—according to this position—that Hugh not only did not understand his own work in the first place, but that, when he tried to improve it, he was incapable of doing so effectively.

Clearly, this was not the case. Aside from the fact that Hugh himself is on record as not being interested in revising his own work,[117] the vast majority of the edits of the second recension are meaningless and contribute little to the clarity of the text one way or another. But, believing that Hugh was responsible for all of these revisions, Sicard tries to find logical arguments for the more intrusive ones.

For example, one practice of the editor was to shorten most of the lists of names in *The Mystic Ark* by implying ellipses, as in the list of the forty-two stopping places of the Hebrews' journey through the desert and the list of popes (Fig. 5, no. 13, no. 4b).[118] The reason Sicard gives for this is that, between the writing of the first recension and the second, Hugh had compiled similar (and, in one case, very slightly more precise) lists in his *Chronicon*, an aid to the study of history that has an extensive collection of such lists; the person using *The Mystic Ark* could then, according to Sicard, turn to the *Chronicon* for this information, since Hugh had already recorded it there.[119] But, one is forced to ask, what would be more likely for a potential twelfth-century user of *The Mystic Ark* to have at hand, Hugh's recently written *Chronicon* or the Book of Numbers, in which the list of the Hebrews' stopping places appears and which, I hesitate to point out, as one of the books of the Bible, was already available at the time of the writing of the first recension? The situation is similar with the list of popes: no medieval scribe, knowing the difficulty of obtaining books—and well-edited ones at that—would ever consider it such an inevitability that the average user of *The Mystic Ark* would have such assumed access to Hugh's *Chronicon* as to make the recording of these names in *The Mystic Ark* redundant. No, the point of the elimination of these lists was one of simple convenience for the copyist and was completely unrelated to Hugh's publication of the *Chronicon*.

Indeed, the general lack of understanding of *The Mystic Ark* found in the revisions shows a fundamental lack of sympathy with the subject that makes it plain that the editor's interest was in reducing his own work rather than in anticipating how the eventual user of *The Mystic Ark* would go about producing the *Ark*. Furthermore, as the *Chronicon* and other of Hugh's writings show, the dropping of these sorts of lists is absolutely contrary to Hugh's working methods, to his pedagogical commitment, and to his view of both history in general and the history of salvation in particular. For the same reasons, Hugh would never have dropped these lists from the painting itself of *The Mystic Ark*, as Sicard claims, contrary though it may be to his own theory of the use of the *Chronicon* lists.[120] Apparently taking his cue not from the first recension but from the second, Sicard thinks that the original painting would only have had the first and last names of lists like that of the stopping places—a series which, it should be pointed out, Hugh considered to be of such importance that he planned to devote a treatise to it alone, explicating it name by name.[121]

Equally indicative of the editor's fundamental lack of understanding of the painting of *The Mystic Ark* is his weak attempt at clarifying problems raised by the careless work of the reporter. In the first recension, the reporter records how, despite the fact that the Ark of Genesis had a length six times its width, the image of the Ark should be shortened to four times so that its form might be "more suitable" (cf. Fig. 7). For the reasons noted above, however, the reporter then reverts to the biblical proportions of a length six times the width.[122] In the second recension, far from correcting the accidental reversion to the biblical proportions, the editor has actually deleted the very important passage on the reduction of the painted Ark—without an awareness of which any newly constructed image would be very awkward indeed—and in its place has uncomprehendingly restored the oversight of the first, something that could only have been done by someone with a fundamental misunderstanding of the reason that the proportions were altered in the first place.[123] This was not Hugh changing his mind, as Sicard thinks.[124]

Even more illustrative of how false premises lead to false conclusions is Sicard's forced explanation of revisions related to the Last Judgment and Hell, changes he describes as among the most significant of the second recension.[125] In the first recension, *The Mystic Ark* is described as having in the eastern tip of the world "Paradise as the Bosom of Abraham" (Fig. 5, no. 11) while the western tip contains "the Judgment of the Universal Resurrection," with angels receiving the elect into "Heaven" on the right (of Christ) and with "Hell" in the northern corner (Fig. 5, no. 16).[126] The second recension omits any reference to the Last Judgment or to the elect being received into Heaven; and while it does refer to Hell, it deletes the description of Hell as being in the north, making it seem as if the entire western tip is now occupied with the depiction of Hell alone. Having once decided that Hugh was personally and directly responsible for both writing the first recension and editing the second, Sicard tries to find support for these changes in Hugh's writings.

According to Sicard, despite the explicit reference to the Bosom of Abraham, this passage refers to the eastern tip of the world as signifying the Garden of Eden alone.[127] The different treatments between the first and second recensions of the western tip came about, he maintains, because they present entirely different views of this aspect of *The Mystic Ark*, views that are the result of Hugh's conceptual development of the subject during the period between the two recensions. According to Sicard, the first recension gives a historical view, with the end of time culminating in the Last Judgment, with its rewards and punishments for the elect and the damned. The second recension, he believes, "maintains the historio-spatial aim attested by the east-west orientation, but its expression is much weakened in favor of a more static representation of the universe given by the position of the elements that compose it: in the one case it sums up the course of universal history, in the other it disposes, according to their hierarchy, the 'places' that at that time constituted the cosmos."[128] Sicard believes that what he sees in the first recension as a succession of Paradise/world/Heaven-and-Hell is replaced in the second by the conceptually more advanced hierarchy of Paradise/world/Hell because of the elimination of Heaven in the west, something that provides a "cosmically" more correct schema of the universe, the expression of which he finds in works of Hugh's that happened to be written after the first recension. But even Sicard himself is dissatisfied with this explanation, being forced to admit that the fundamental logic of the symmetry of the works of creation in the east and the final outcome of the works of restoration in the west—one of the most fundamental and constant aspects of Hugh's thought and the basis of his later *De Sacramentis*—is completely lost, and that the two different conceptions presented by the two different recensions are irreconcilable.[129]

There are many problems with this interpretation, not the least of which is that, in this case, the best place to look for an explanation of the issues involved is within the image of *The Mystic Ark* itself, not outside of it. To begin with, the reporter did not describe the Garden of Eden in terms of the Bosom of Abraham without reason, and that reason is that the image overtly functions in a complex, multivalent manner, referring to both the Garden of Eden and something more. This is a subject that is fully taken up in my later study. For now, let me just say that, in the Fathers, the term "the Bosom of Abraham" is often used to refer to the *limbus Patrum*, that place where the souls of the just who lived before the Incarnation await the coming of Christ—a place that Augustine, for one, repeatedly calls both "the Bosom of Abraham" and "Paradise," and that others located in the Garden of Eden.[130] Compositionally, it appears on the line of generation before the Incarnation of the central cubit because the *limbus Patrum* was necessary only before Christ's coming, not after; it appears before the beginning of human history (the sixth day) because its inhabitants were removed from that history, from time. Conceptually, the Bosom of Abraham in *The Mystic Ark* has to do with the polemical controversy in which Hugh was engaged with Abelard around the time of the inception of the *Ark* lectures. Although Hugh (and Bernard) may have exaggerated Abelard's position, they asserted that he claimed a spiritual superiority for the just of the Old Testament over those who came after the Incarnation.[131] In giving such a visually prominent place to such a theologically secondary concept, Hugh is polemically engaging Abelard by emphasizing the primacy of the sacraments of grace over those of natural and the written law, making it plain that the latter were not able to allow those just who came before the Incarnation "to enter the gate of the kingdom of heaven." Although in a state of spiritual happiness, they are excluded from the vision of God—depicted in *The Mystic Ark* above the cosmos as the crowning component of the painting—until the sacrifice of Christ, the greatest of the sacraments of grace, represented in *The Mystic Ark* by the central cubit.

As to Sicard's idea that the first recension localizes heaven in the western tip of the world because the saved of the Last Judgment (which takes place there) are described as being received into heaven, this is simply not the case. The Last Judgment, by definition, must include the saved. Their location in the composition of *The Mystic Ark* at the terminus of the chronological sequence of the line of generation is strictly an indication of the outcome of the history of salvation and of the end of time, not of Heaven's locality. Heaven is clearly described as being right where it is always traditionally understood as being, above the ethereal zone mentioned above, where the nine choirs of angels perpetually worship God (Fig. 2, no. 4).

In the end, the cosmic schema presented by Hugh in both recensions of *The Mystic Ark* is traditional in its basic structure of celestial paradise (in the choirs of angels, not the paradise of the Garden of Eden or the *limbus Patrum*)/world/hell.[132] There is no development of Hugh's conception of the structure of the cosmos here.

But back to the confusion caused by the editor of the second recension. His elimination of the Last Judgment, leaving only the torments of Hell, is not the most important revision of the second recension, as Sicard would have it, but the most inexplicable. It is entirely contrary to Hugh's thinking on the history of salvation, the main lines of which consist of the works of creation and of restoration, the latter concluding with the final work of restoration, the Last Judgment, at which the elect as a community are at long last restored to their creator, the ultimate outcome of the history of salvation.[133] Furthermore, the western tip in which all of this takes place is at the end of historical time, according to the line of generation of the Ark; in this regard, it should be pointed out that it is not Hell that marks the end of time, but the Last Judgment. To delete the Last Judgment from the text of *The Mystic Ark* is essentially to deny the chronological structure that forms the conceptual core and compositional central axis of *The Mystic Ark*. Far from being by Hugh, it seems that this deeply ignorant "revision" came about because of the editor's complete lack of personal engagement with his subject. In the first recension, it is said that

> The other tip, which projects toward the west, has the Judgment of the Universal Resurrection with the elect on the right and the rejected on the left. In the northern corner of this tip is Hell, into which the damned are thrust along with the apostate spirits.[134]

To a person as clearly out of touch with *The Mystic Ark* as the editor of the second recension is, this would be a very perplexing passage. It is traditional for the elect to be on the right hand of Christ and the damned on his left. But to have Hell specifically described as being in the north in the painting of *The Mystic Ark*—that is, on the right hand of Christ—seems to have been beyond the editor's comprehension, and he reacted as he did throughout his revision when he came across something that confused him: he simply removed it, just as he did with the seasonal component of the quaternary harmony. Seemingly left with the choice of eliminating either the Last Judgment or Hell in his misguided attempt at increasing clarity, he opted for removing the Last Judgment, apparently preferring to satisfy the medieval imperative of antithesis, in this case opposing Hell to Heaven, which is quite prominently indicated by the choirs of angels on either side of the head of the Lord at the top of the painting. This also allowed him to remove the reference to the locality of Hell as in the north, something that clearly bothered him. But while Hell is not often depicted as in the north (or on the right hand of Christ) in art, it is often associated with the north in literature. In *The Mystic Ark*, it is specified as being in the north both because of the traditional association of the north with ignorance and evil—the north is the place of "the fellowship of the devil" in *The Mystic Ark*—and because it directly relates to Hugh's sequence of descent away from the redeemer in the central cubit, the ascent of the northwest corner being the final descent, descending into the Blindness of Ignorance, which is spiritual death (Fig. 8).[135] Having eliminated the Last Judgment, the editor dropped the scroll and scepter held by the Majesty with their all-important passages from Matthew 25 as well—"Come, you who have been blessed by my Father . . ." and "Depart from me, you who have been cursed . . ."—since they now made less sense.[136] Contrary to Sicard's idea of the evolving nature of Hugh's thought, however, these very passages appear as culminating elements of his conception of the Last Judgment in his *De sacramentis*, a work that postdates *The Mystic Ark* and stands as his final word on such matters.[137]

But the list of uncomprehending revisions in the second recension goes on. As if in confirmation of the misapprehending and careless nature of these previous changes—rather than any more profound reason—the editor drops the phrase *et quasi in solio sedens*, "as if sitting on a throne," from the description of the Majesty in the second recension.[138] This is an edit that, along with the deletion of the Matthew 25 passages, reduces the entire description of the Majesty to one sentence in the second recension, although the Majesty is visually the most dominant component of the entire composition. Sicard would like to think that this was because of the great subtlety of the editor, that, having eliminated the Last Judgment, his iconographical sense was so acute that he felt compelled to drop the reference to the throne on which the Majesty sits—as if it were a throne of judgment—even though it is barely visible (Fig. 2, no. 2). The imagery of the throne, however, is a fundamental part of the Majesty's iconographical conception, which is based on the vision of Isaiah (Isaiah 6) and which plays a principal part in both *The Moral Ark* and *The Mystic Ark*. Indeed, it is the correlation of the Majesty with the vision of Isaiah with which Hugh begins his discussion of the painting of *The Mystic Ark* in *The Moral Ark*.[139] Sicard, forced to acknowledge the absolute centrality of the vision of Isaiah in *The Moral Ark*, attempts to extricate himself from this contradiction by saying that while the throne does not refer to judgment in *The Moral Ark*, it does in the first recension of *The Mystic Ark*—even though he repeatedly states throughout his work that the painting referred to in *The Moral Ark* is that of *The Mystic Ark*.[140] This distinction between the thrones is, of course, not the case. The Majesty of *The Mystic Ark* is the same Majesty of *The Moral Ark*, and he is explicitly based on the vision of Isaiah, as indicated by the two seraphim whose wings cover his face and feet and whom the editor of the second recension did not remove.[141] The meaning of the throne is the same in both, which is not judgment in either case: heaven is the throne of the Lord, just as stated in Isaiah, as noted in the commentaries on the vision of Isaiah, and as implied by the "heavens" or cosmos that the Lord holds in front of himself in *The Mystic Ark*.[142] In fact, shortly after the deleted reference to the throne is another reference to it that is not deleted, leaving the reader to wonder—given the clear basis in the vision of Isaiah—if this is a fully thought-out revision based on a major change of conception contrary to Hugh's own thought, or if it is simply more careless work, the pattern for which is fully established.[143]

Even more convoluted is Sicard's argument regarding the use of color in the vertical system of the three stages of the Ark, which have a correspondence to the horizontal system of planks of the three periods of the history of salvation (Figs. 4 and 11). Earlier, I argued against Sicard's idea that the imagery of the three periods was not present in the original painting of *The Mystic Ark*, with Sicard claiming that *The Moral Ark* represents the state of the original painting and that the text of *The Mystic Ark* describes a later version.[144] Sicard also thinks that there was a change in Hugh's conception of the use of color between the first and second recensions of *The Mystic Ark*.[145] He feels that, in the first recension, the text—which specifies the color of only one stage and which I will explain fully in a moment—indicates that the first stage is to be colored "red" (incidentally, mistranslating *purpureus* as *rouge* and so ignoring the highly charged symbolism of purple as referring to both royalty and sacrificial blood).[146] In the second recension, he believes that a fundamental change of conception has come about that requires all three of the vertical stages to be colored purple (or "red," as he says).

This interpretation, however, is based on a straightforward misunderstanding of the language of the passage in question. When the text of the first recension says, "Purple should be used where the people of grace are located within," Sicard misinterprets it to mean that the first stage is meant to be purple.[147] His reason for this is that, since purple is the color of grace, which is the life of the Church, this is appropriate for the first stage since this life "extends the Church and constitutes it." This first recension passage on coloring is so unclear that the editor of the second recension—as was his practice—simply dropped the entire thing, saying only that "The Ark is painted with the color purple and the surface of the earth is painted with the color green."[148] The reason for this change, as Sicard sees it, is that Hugh had come to realize by the time of the second recension that such a thing would be in "greater conformity with [his own] ecclesiology"; since purple is the color of grace, and grace and the Church are co-extensive, this should be shown to animate the entire Church, "not just those of the first stage, but also, *a fortiori*, those who . . . are in the second or third stage." In support of his idea of conceptual change on the part of Hugh, Sicard cites a passage found in Hugh's *Dialogus* that he believes was written sometime between the first and second recensions and in which Hugh repeats his idea from *The Mystic Ark* that from the beginning of time there were always people of grace in every period, very slightly elaborating upon the role of grace in this passage.[149] But, contrary to what Sicard would like to think, this passage from the *Dialogus* is essentially no different in regard to the issues at play in *The Mystic Ark* and, in any event, does not provide an intellectual justification for an expansion of purple throughout the three stages, something that would be both fundamentally contrary to the very concept of the vertical stage scheme and redundant in regard to the much more articulate expression of the idea of people of grace in every period in the horizontal plank system. Although he acknowledges Hugh's "preoccupation with theological and spiritual order," he sees this crude contradiction and redundancy as "progress," as "clearer," and as "happily simplifying a drawing already quite complex."

In Sicard's defense, the text of the first recension is horrendous. But his real problem lies not so much with this nightmarish text as with the practice of interpreting the thoughtless mistakes of the careless reporter of the first recension and those of the unengaged editor of the second as serious intellectual positions of Hugh's, the greatest living theologian of Europe.

What is clear about the first recension, however, is how the color system of the planks works. The length of the Ark is the historical existence of the Church. To express its progress from the beginning of time until the end, the horizontal progression of the Ark is divided into three periods: the period of natural law, the period of the written law, and the period of grace. Coordinated with these three periods is a system of three "planks" that runs the length of both sides of the Ark. Each plank represents one of the three different types of people (of nature, of the law, or of grace); and the particular grouping of the three in any given period indicates the level of prominence of each type in that period. While each period is by definition dominated by the people of that period, people of the other two types are shown to exist alongside them. For example, in the period of natural law, there were also people of the written law and of grace. But the people of natural law were in the ascendancy, those of the written law were the second most populous, and those of grace the least. In the period of the written law, the latter were dominant, while the people of grace were the next, and the people of natural law the least. Continuing in this fashion, in the period of grace, the people of grace hold the first place, the people of natural law the second, and the people of the written law the third. To express this visually, the three planks are varied in arrangement and width in each period, with the plank of the predominant people toward the outside of the Ark, that of the second most populous people toward the inside, and that of least between the two (being "pressed" between them, as the reporter puts it).[150]

What is less clear in the first recension is how the color system of the stages works, and I hope that the reader will pay closer attention to its details than the reporter and the editor did. The three stages of the Ark correspond to, among other things, the basic concepts that underlie the three periods: nature, law, and grace. Thus, there is a macrocosmic horizontal historical progression from one period to another (the three periods), and a microcosmic vertical spiritual progression from one spiritual state to another (the three stages). Typically, Hugh sought to integrate these two components—one of the characteristics of *The Mystic Ark* that makes it so great. But Hugh, like Bernard of Clairvaux—and unlike the reporter and the editor—normally considered the full ramifications of whatever subject was at hand. And this is where the origin of the difficulty with the color system of the three stages lies.

The reporter of the first recension says about the color system of the stages:

> The Ark—which is painted on the surface within with various colors according to the differentiation of the stages—ought not to be painted with the color green in that part where the people of natural law are situated within, nor with yellow where the people of the written law are within. Purple, however, should be used where the people of grace are located within so that one may employ color in the same way in which the surface of the earth outside corresponds to the people of natural law through the color green, so that here alone a likeness functions within between the two.[151]

What this means—and the reader may be excused if he or she had a little difficulty with this piece, which is clearly by a less articulate writer than Hugh—is that, aside from the macrocosmic color system of the planks, there should also be a microcosmic color system "within" (that is, between the twin systems of planks) for the stages. However, a color problem arises because of the difficulties of reconciling the macrocosmic horizontal system with the microcosmic vertical. In that special form of awkwardness reserved for those who are in over their heads, the reporter tries to explain this problem negatively. That is, he says not what the colors should be, generally speaking, but what they should not be—aware, however unclearly he expresses it, that the issue is not so much what they are, as what they cannot be. Thus the Ark "ought not to be painted with the color green in that part where people of natural law (as microcosmic individuals, not macrocosmic nations or cultures) are situated within"; and where they are "within" the Ark—that is, "within" or between the twin system of planks—is in the first stage, which is marked with the inscription *Nature* (Figs. 4 and 11). Nor should the Ark be painted "with yellow where the people of the written law are within": in the second stage, which is marked with the inscription *Law* (again, this is meant in the microcosmic sense of the individual, not a nation or culture). The most obvious reason that green and yellow are not appropriate for the first and second stages is that these stages visually continue beyond the central cubit, toward the end of time. Unlike the horizontal planks that indicate the different types of people (in the macrocosmic sense) in all periods, such a color system in the vertical stages would visually compromise the clarity of the horizontal system, seemingly indicating that the Christian conception of the period of the written law asserted itself beyond the coming of Christ and that the period of natural law will again be dominant at the end of time. But there is another reason as well, and this is that green and yellow are not appropriate in that, to use the language of *The Mystic Ark*, each color "is in the composition of the Ark, but it is not like the Ark";[152] that is, individuals of the spiritual levels of the stages (as opposed to the historical periods of the planks) of natural law or the written law may be in the Church, but their spiritual level does not equate in any way with the spirituality of the Church.[153]

Purple is a different story. It "should be used where the people of grace are located within"; that is, in the third stage, marked *Grace*. The reason for this is "so that one may employ color *in the same way* in which the surface of the earth outside corresponds to the people of natural law through the color green." This is an awkward way of saying that just as the green of the system of planks relates what it stands for (the people of natural law) to the green of the world in the *mappa mundi* in the sense of that which is of this world and extrinsic to the Ark or Church, so the purple of the system of planks relates what it stands for (the people of grace) to the purple of the third stage, grace, which is that which is most intrinsic to the Church. To drive home the irregularity of the arrangement of the color system of the stages, the reporter makes a point of noting that "here alone a likeness functions within between the two"—that is, it is only with the third stage that there is a color relationship between one of the colors of the plank system and one of the colors of the stage system.

Hugh not only had a "preoccupation with theological and spiritual order," as Sicard noted, he is on record as advocating the use of color in pedagogical systems.[154] Though the color system here is very poorly described by the reporter, Sicard's reading of the text of the first recension to mean that purple was appropriate for the first stage would have been inconceivable to Hugh. Each of the three stages is clearly marked with its respective principle of the three periods: nature, law, and grace. To color the first stage, the stage of nature, purple would not only be to deny the basic meaning of that stage, it would be to deny the principle of vertical spiritual ascent toward the divine (where one attains the highest spiritual level only at the top), which would contradict the teaching and the methodology, respectively, of Hugh. Sicard has badly confused the vertical and horizontal systems that are at the heart of *The Mystic Ark*.

As to the first and second stages, the reporter of the first recension clearly states that they are to be painted but does not specify the colors (except to say that they are not to be green or yellow). While this leaves us to assume that they are nonsymbolic, he could just as easily have neglected to mention what that symbolism is.

The color passage of the first recension is unquestionably a mess, and this is why the editor of the second recension tried to revise it. But it was beyond him, and he simply accepted purple as the only stated color for that part of the Ark between the system of planks and lamely referred to the use of green for the earth without any further reference to color relationships or meaning.[155] The rest he just dropped: blind to the system of spiritual levels, deaf to the elaborate interrelation of the horizontal and vertical progressions, and mute regarding the color relationship between the third stage and the plank system. Far from there being a subtle change of intellectual conception between the first and second recensions, the editor of the second recension never really understood the poorly expressed color system of the first recension, and his revision is indicative only of his ready willingness to eliminate whatever he could not understand.

Hugh closed *The Moral Ark* with the statement, "There is still more that I might have said if I were not afraid of wearying you."[156] I wish I had the luxury of being able to say the same thing, but there is still one more misinterpretation that I am obliged to take up in regard to Sicard's views of the second recension, though it is by no means his last. As with the component of the three periods of the history of salvation, I have already argued against Sicard's idea that the crucial quaternary harmony was not present in the original painting of *The Mystic Ark* (Fig. 2, no. 9, Fig. 9).[157] Sicard also thinks that Hugh—about whom it was said by one of his contemporaries, "In all of the Latin Church, there is no one to be found who can compare to him in wisdom"[158]—having done such a miserable job of copying someone else's work on the harmony of the seasons into his own text in the first recension, was so dull that he was unable to correct a very minor mistake (simply a question of verbally reorienting the seasonal harmony within the quaternary harmony by a quarter turn) and felt compelled to drop the passage entirely in the second.[159] Even more, according to Sicard, Hugh also felt obliged to drop the passage on the harmony of the qualities (hot, cold, moist, and dry) that immediately follows that on the seasons. The reason Sicard gives for this additional cut is that the passage on the qualities is part of a discussion of the harmony of the cosmos that is based in part on the harmony of the seasons, whose confused and confusing passage had been deleted. But, in fact, the confusing part alone of the seasonal harmony was removed by the editor of the second recension; the main discussion of the seasons (which coordinates them with the four cardinal directions) remained fundamentally untouched. The unclear passage on the seasons is, actually, mildly redundant and not truly necessary at all (unlike the deleted instruction that the Signs of the Zodiac should be oriented with Aries at the top, which was cut out as well[160]). Thus, in the deletion of the harmony of the seasons, there was no reason to drop the passage on the harmony of the qualities. That is, there was no logical reason, for the real motivation was guilt by association: it happened to be associated with the unclear passage and it was removed simply through the inertia of intellectual indifference.

There was, therefore, no continuing change from the original painting of *The Mystic Ark* to the *reportatio* of *The Mystic Ark*. *The Moral Ark* does not represent the original state of the painting, but rather was considered to be the most original part of the *Ark* lectures, a series of lectures that was meant to be loose by conscious design.[161] *The Moral Ark* is under no obligation to recount literally the image from which its thought took its impetus. Nor is there any need to explain the differences between the first and second recensions of *The Mystic Ark* as a continuing change of intellectual conception, especially when such an explanation implies direct authorship by Hugh. The revisions of the second recension are characterized by a lack of personal engagement with the subject, an unreflective elimination of whatever the editor did not understand, an unseemly desire to reduce the amount of text that had to be copied, and an ignorance of the polemical context of *The Mystic Ark*. Furthermore, it is quite clear that the editor was oblivious to the summa-like comprehensiveness of *The Mystic Ark* and its almost complete interconnecting coherency, both of which are as much a part of its content in the narrow sense of the word as they are a part of its meaning in the broader sense.

3. THE EDITING OF THE SECOND RECENSION

The conclusions to the previous section raise two interrelated questions: To what degree can we be certain of the chronology of *The Mystic Ark*? And why was the editor of the second recension so personally disengaged from his work?

Earlier, I gave my reasons for accepting as likely van den Eynde's general grouping of works related to *The Moral Ark* and *The Mystic Ark* while questioning the relative order within it.[162] Although the general methodology of establishing relative chronologies between different texts on the basis of conceptual development is certainly legitimate, the specific natures of the writings under consideration in the group related to *The Moral Ark* and *The Mystic Ark* do not lend themselves well to this type of analysis. The evidence is simply not there to support van den Eynde's dating of *The Moral Ark* to shortly before 1127 (his date for the *Sententie de divinitate*) or of *The Mystic Ark* to 1128 or 1129. There is far less evidence to support Sicard's suggestion that there was a gap from one to two years between the original lectures and *The Moral Ark*, from two to four years between the original lectures and *The Mystic Ark*, or from one to three years between *The Moral Ark* and *The Mystic Ark*.[163]

Until further scholarship more precisely establishes sounder relative and absolute chronologies, all that can be said with certainty is that *The Mystic Ark* was written sometime from 1125 to early 1130. The evidence for an absolute chronology is indirect but compelling: the terminal entry in the list of papal regnancies in *The Mystic Ark* is Honorius II, who reigned from December 21, 1124 to February 13, 1130, something that suggests that the first recension must date from 1125 to early 1130.[164] The exchange of letters between Hugh and Bernard in the Abelard affair tends to confirm this, with Bernard's *Letter* 77—for which he apologizes as a late response to a previous letter by Hugh, though how late we do not know—variously dated from 1125 to 1128.[165] As to relative chronology, the unusual statement recognizing its popularity with which *The Moral Ark* begins suggests that *The Moral Ark* was written soon after the original lectures in response to that popularity.[166] There is no reason to think that *The Mystic Ark* was written much later: it refers to *The Moral Ark* and quotes from it, but *The Mystic Ark* is in no way posterior to it in a developmental sense. The fact that *The Mystic Ark* is a *reportatio* implies that the reporter was a participant in the original lectures, which in turn suggests a composition soon after the lectures and in all likelihood immediately after *The Moral Ark*, probably as part of an initial burst of enthusiasm.

As to the dating of the second recension, the failure of Sicard's textual analysis renders his dating of around 1135 completely unsupportable.[167] What is of interest about the second recension in regard to chronology is the elimination of the reference to a planned treatise on the forty-two stopping places of the Hebrews' journey through the desert: since this treatise was never written, the deletion raises the possibility, at least, that the deletion—and so the second recension—took place after the death of Hugh (February 11, 1141).[168]

It is at this point that the question of why the editor of the second recension was so personally disengaged from his work ties in with that of the chronology of the second recension. Sicard has pointed out a pattern of usage for the first and second recensions. It was the first recension that Saint Victor itself used when it wanted to make new copies; two manuscripts of *The Mystic Ark* have survived from Saint Victor itself, one from around 1140 to 1150 and the other from 1220 to 1255, both of them first recension.[169] Furthermore, places with which Saint Victor maintained strong relations also had first recension copies of *The Mystic Ark*. Bernard's monastery, Clairvaux, was one of these; and there was a web of English connections, probably established through former canons, teachers, and students of Saint Victor, possibly Andrew of Saint Victor, Robert of Melun, Laurence of Westminster, and others.[170] What Sicard has failed to notice is the significance of all this.

Clearly, it was the first recension that was seen by Saint Victor itself as inherently the more authoritative of the two. And it was the first recension that had an immediate but short diffusion.[171] Yet it was the second recension—the less authoritative, which, far from being an improvement on the first, shows a real lack of personal engagement with the subject—that became the most widespread. How could such a situation have come about? Why was Saint Victor using the first recension in the thirteenth century, long after the death of Hugh and long after the second recension had been made and established as the more common prototype? Why did institutions with close ties to Saint Victor generally have copies of the first recension, while other, less closely related places generally had the second?

The reason that Sicard gives for the impetus of the second recension is the great popularity of *The Mystic Ark*, this popularity suggesting such an improved edition to Hugh because of the carelessness of the first.[172] Sicard, however, finds himself caught in the contradiction discussed above, which even he recognizes: that the second recension is, in fact, not an improvement on the first at all. Even so, the impetus for the second recension was indeed the great popularity of the first, though it was not revised by Hugh, as I believe I have shown. It seems that it was the particular scriptorium practice of Saint Victor that was responsible for the pattern of both the first and the second recensions apparently originally stemming from Saint Victor, with the first having an aspect of production for "in-house" use, while the second could, in consequence, be said to have an aspect of production for external consumption.

The twelfth-century *Liber ordinis* of Saint Victor (the book of customs) stipulates, regarding the duties of the *armarius* or librarian, who oversaw the scriptorium,

> All writings that are made in the community—whether inside or outside [the monastery]—are the responsibility of his office to the effect that he himself ought to provide the scribes with parchment and the other things that are necessary for writing, and that he himself should hire those who write for pay.[173]

A number of recent studies on the textual and artistic production of the scriptorium of Saint Victor have drawn attention to the practice referred to in this passage of hiring out work that could not be taken care of by the collegial scriptorium within the monastery to commercial scribes outside.[174] Every effort seems to have been made to ensure a high standard of work within the collegial scriptorium, with permission being necessary from the abbot himself for the appointment of canon-scribes and with access to the scriptorium severely restricted to limit distraction.[175] As a new collegial house especially devoted to learning and teaching, Saint Victor had embarked on an ambitious campaign of building up its own library—not those of other institutions—as fast as possible.[176] At the same time, it performed extensive duties for the royal chancery and even for the Bishop of Paris. It was because of these unusual burdens on the internal scriptorium that the *armarius* had to go outside the walls for additional scribal help. It is known that commercial copyists had begun to work in Paris at just this time, and that those who worked for Saint Victor also worked for a number of other Parisian monasteries.[177] But the customs of Saint Victor offer no information about quality control over the work sent outside the monastery to these commercial copyists, except to say that the *armarius* was responsible for it.

We do not know who the editor of the second recension was. But we do know a few things about him. He was personally disengaged from the concept of *The Mystic Ark*, his subject. He was, in practice, indifferent to any real improvement of the text if this involved actually understanding it. What can only be described as ignorance of the principles of the quaternary harmony suggest that he was poorly educated (or perhaps unsuccessfully educated is better) for someone who was a scribe. Perhaps most striking of all, he displays a total lack of familiarity with the work of Hugh, a scholar who established a school of thought at Saint Victor in the sense described by R. W. Southern, whose work continued to elicit enormous interest long after his death, and of whom his community was immensely proud.[178] And the evidence suggests—in the restoration of the biblical proportions of the Ark, in the elimination of the previously mentioned passage concerning the quaternary harmony, in the mistake regarding the color system of the stages—that the editor of the second recension had no visual access to the painting. This could have been either because he was not allowed into that part of the monastery where Hugh taught or because the painting was no longer extant. But even if this were the case, it would then suggest that the editor had no convenient access to canons who actually understood *The Mystic Ark* through the lectures, the painting, or the text. All this makes it fairly inconceivable that a canon regular of Saint Victor acted as the editor of the second recension—and very probably that it was a commercial scribe to whom *The Mystic Ark* was hired out for a new recension to deal with the great interest that continued to be shown in it. It seems that it was this new recension that was copied, apparently by external scribes, when requests were made from institutions other than those that had unusually strong relations with Saint Victor: for example, as seems to have been the case with Saint Albans, whose twelfth-century, second recension copy of *The Mystic Ark*, probably requested by Abbot Simon of Saint Albans, is now held in Oxford.[179] And it appears that it was the first recension that was used by the internal scriptorium for copies for Saint Victor and its closest friends: such as Clairvaux, whose twelfth-century, first recension copy of the *Ark* is now in Troyes.[180]

The evidence of the second recension suggests that this revision was made after the death of Hugh. I have already noted that the deletion from the second recension of a reference to a proposed book by Hugh on the forty-two stopping places of the Hebrews' journey through the desert tends to support this view. The *Indiculum*, a fifteenth-century copy of a bibliography of Hugh's work made on the command of Abbot Gilduin of Saint Victor shortly after Hugh's death, does as well. In it, in the entry for *The Mystic Ark*, there is a reference to chapter headings, but the space for the actual headings themselves was left blank,[181] something that suggests there were expectations that such headings, which are absent from the first recension, would be made fairly soon. It may be that headings were expected to be made as part of the second recension and that the second recension was done around this time, shortly after the death of Hugh. If so, the fact that these headings were never made is in perfect accord with the consistently abysmal work done by the editor and his complete lack of personal engagement.

Chapter Three

THE NATURE AND ORIGINAL FUNCTION OF THE TEXT OF *THE MYSTIC ARK*

While the likelihood that the editor was a commercial scribe may explain his lack of personal engagement with this spiritual text that was meant for group discussion, it does not explain why poor work in general was tolerated for *The Mystic Ark*—either the fairly mediocre first recension by a student of Saint Victor, or the truly inadequate second recension apparently by an outside scribe, neither of whom were models of their professions. The conclusion is inescapable that this was the case because *The Mystic Ark* was not considered to be a literary piece.

As to the first recension, it was a *reportatio*: the fact that it was not personally written by Hugh but by a student, whether internal or external, certainly put the work in a different category of editorial attention, however popular it was. But there is more to it, since the text was never given a proper title or, what is more, an explanatory preface.[182] Regarding the second recension, the casual attitude toward it seems to be the result of the knowledge on the part of the editor that *The Mystic Ark* was a *reportatio*, and a flawed one at that; it was not by Hugh and need not be treated with the deference normally shown to the writing of a respected author. This attitude was not helped by an expansion of the work of the scriptorium from 1140 to 1150 so great that fully one-third of Saint Victor's twelfth-century manuscript collection was copied at this time (with a noticeable increase in the number of hands beginning in 1135),[183] precisely the time during which I suggest the second recension was made.

But, again, the real reason that the text received only incidental editorial attention—and perhaps the principal reason that Hugh had allowed a student to write the *reportatio* in the first place rather than doing it himself—was that, by its very genre, it was not considered to be a literary piece, properly speaking.

1. THE SUPPOSITION THAT THE TEXT OF *THE MYSTIC ARK* WAS ORIGINALLY INTENDED AS AN APPENDIX TO *THE MORAL ARK*

In the manuscript tradition, whenever *The Mystic Ark* is found, it and the treatise of *The Moral Ark* virtually always accompany each other, although not in a consistent fashion.[184] Sicard's second basic error of interpretation—as mentioned earlier, his failure to recognize the basically simple relationship between the painting of *The Mystic Ark*, the treatise of *The Moral Ark*, and the *reportatio* of *The Mystic Ark*—has caused him to further misinterpret the nature and original function of *The Mystic Ark*.

The evidence that the texts themselves offer is certainly not straightforward. I have already noted the confusion caused by the absence of an explanatory preface to *The Mystic Ark*. This lack of clarity has been greatly compounded by *The Moral Ark*, which in the manuscript tradition has no less than seven different closings that are repeated more than once, and an additional four unique closings. These have been recognized to one degree or another by a number of scholars, but most completely by Sicard.[185] The original closing (ending in *edificatam esse leteris*) is the fullest; this is a proper ending that brings the writing to an overt close, but which does so by referring to the painting of *The Mystic Ark*—a painting that had been referred to earlier in *The Moral Ark* but that is not actually necessary at all for understanding this treatise and that plays only a very small part in it:

> I was going to speak briefly, but I admit that I was glad to have had so much to say to you. And, in fact, there is still more that I might have said if I were not afraid of wearying you (*fastidium non timerem*). Therefore, let us now propose the exemplar of our Ark itself, as we have promised. This we have painted externally in order that you may learn from without what you ought to do within so that, when you have reproduced a form of this exemplar in your heart, you may rejoice that the house of God has been built within you (*edificatam esse leteris*).[186]

This is by far the most common of the closings, being found in 84 of the 143 complete copies of *The Moral Ark* listed in Sicard's painstaking study of the manuscript tradition of the Ark. More significantly, it is the one employed in the copies of *The Moral Ark* that accompany the two surviving first recension versions of *The Mystic Ark* from Saint Victor itself.[187]

The second most common closing (ending in *fastidium non timerem*), of which there are thirty-three examples, drops the reference to the painting of *The Mystic Ark*, ending somewhat awkwardly on Hugh's concern with wearying his readers. The various other endings, none of which come anywhere near the first two in number, are no less clumsy.

At the same time, although copies of *The Mystic Ark* are virtually always found in sequence with *The Moral Ark*, the order of sequence is not standard. While *The Mystic Ark* is most commonly found immediately following *The Moral Ark*, at other times it immediately precedes *The Moral Ark*. The latter is the case, significantly, both in the crucial copies from Saint Victor and in the order indicated in the *Indiculum* of Saint Victor.[188] When *The Mystic Ark* precedes *The Moral Ark*, the distinction between the two is unquestioned, with a proper closing to *The Mystic Ark* and a proper title and preface to *The Moral Ark*. But when *The Mystic Ark* follows *The Moral Ark*, the relationship lacks any standard principle: now being incorporated into *The Moral Ark*, now being presented either in a distinct but not independent manner, and now accompanying *The Moral Ark* autonomously, the latter two forms being the more common.[189] Sicard, however, has shown that the two writings were originally distinct and that any alterations in this presentation were made by later copyists, even if very early on. Likewise, closings other than the fullest (*edificatam esse leteris*) were the result of later, although also often quite early, scribal decisions and were not part of the original text; nor were these variations prior to the text of *The Mystic Ark*.

Sicard argues against the earlier idea that *The Mystic Ark*, when following *The Moral Ark*, was originally considered to be a chapter of *The Moral Ark*, a theory he fully refutes. Instead, he characterizes *The Mystic Ark* primarily as an "appendix" to *The Moral Ark* (in part because it has no proper title), which in turn is an "introduction" to *The Mystic Ark*, the latter needing the original closing of *The Moral Ark* because the preface-less *Mystic Ark* is not self-explanatory.[190] The purpose of this "appendix" was to produce *The Mystic Ark*, although the text was consciously meant to be read for its own sake, as Sicard sees it. In contrast to the earlier view of *The Mystic Ark* as a chapter of *The Moral Ark*, he feels that the reason for the sequence found at Saint Victor—with *The Mystic Ark* preceding *The Moral Ark*, and which he seems to see as a form of only secondary importance—was to enable the reader to form a mental picture of *The Mystic Ark* before reading *The Moral Ark*, though it also served to aid in the production of the painting of *The Mystic Ark*. More generally, he sees the painting of *The Mystic Ark* as an illustration of *The Moral Ark* (as opposed to seeing *The Moral Ark* as the most original part of the discussions that came out of the much broader discussions based on the painting of *The Mystic Ark*); he believes that *The Mystic Ark* offers in figural form what *The Moral Ark* presents in verbal form; and he thinks that the verbal form of *The Mystic Ark* is given in place of an actual illustration because it would have been too difficult to produce and preserve such a necessarily large image on parchment.[191]

While Sicard's technical observations regarding the manuscript tradition of *The Mystic Ark* seem sound, the conclusions he draws from these observations are misleading. To accept the more widespread though less authoritative and not original practice of placing *The Mystic Ark* after *The Moral Ark*, a practice that was extrinsic to Saint Victor, as the primary basis for explaining the original nature of *The Mystic Ark*—by which I mean as conceived of at Saint Victor at the time of Hugh—can only further cloud the already murky waters of *The Mystic Ark*. How *The Mystic Ark* was seen after its original conception is of interest, but in this case largely in the sense of explaining a manuscript tradition that was forced to adapt to the inadequacies of the *reportatio*, not in any deeper way. The more authoritative evidence—the manuscript copies of Saint Victor and the *Indiculum*—indicates that, at Saint Victor in the time of Hugh, *The Mystic Ark* was conceived of as preceding *The Moral Ark*, and that in this form *The Mystic Ark* did not have a proper title, or preface, or section headings. This indicates that *The Mystic Ark* was never originally thought of as an "appendix." By the same token, *The Moral Ark* could not have originally (at Saint Victor and in the time of Hugh) been conceived of as an "introduction" to *The Mystic Ark*, since it was *The Mystic Ark* that preceded *The Moral Ark*, which in any event mentions the painting of *The Mystic Ark* several times in the course of discussion. To describe *The Moral Ark* as an introduction to *The Mystic Ark* as Sicard has done is both to misunderstand the significance of the relationship as found in the original sequence and to misrepresent this relationship as found in the later sequence.

Nor does *The Mystic Ark* offer in figural form what *The Moral Ark* presents in verbal form; *The Mystic Ark* is not an illustration of *The Moral Ark*, properly speaking, but rather *The Moral Ark* is the most original part of the *Ark* lectures, and corresponds to the painting of *The Mystic Ark* only as a subset of a much broader whole. Many components that are of the greatest importance in *The Mystic Ark* receive an entirely different emphasis in *The Moral Ark* or are not even referred to at all: the central cubit, the Lamb of God, the ascents and ladders, the quaternary harmony, the Winds, the Months, the Zodiac, the angelic orders, and so on. Similarly, *The Moral Ark* spends an inordinate amount of time on subjects that are not a part of the text or painting of *The Mystic Ark*, such as an entire chapter (out of a total of only four) on the Tree of Life—a Tree of Life that is strongly related to components of *The Mystic Ark* but that is quite different from the Tree of Life as described in *The Mystic Ark*.[192] And at least one major aspect of the *Ark* lectures, the subject of the Ark of Mother Grace, is not discussed at all in *The Moral Ark*.[193] This insistence that *The Mystic Ark* should not be thought of as a description of *The Moral Ark* because *The Moral Ark* is a subset of *The Mystic Ark* is more than a rhetorical fine point: the differences just mentioned were not caused by any continuing change, as Sicard would have it, but are the result of the nature of the relationship of the two texts, as discussed further on.

As to the idea that the text of *The Mystic Ark* acted as a substitute for an actual image that was too difficult both to produce and to preserve, this misconception is related to the very nature and original function of *The Mystic Ark*. A complex issue in light of the state of the secondary literature, this will be a continuing point of discussion in this study. For now, it is enough to say that *The Mystic Ark* is more than a description of an image, and more than the directions for creating an image. It is, more accurately, a body of information that was intended to enable others to undertake, in a relatively independent way, discussions based on the same material as the *Ark* lectures and discussions led by Hugh at Saint Victor. It did this by providing a basic understanding of the individual components of the *Ark*, although not of how it all interacted. Thus, even if some individuals may have read *The Mystic Ark* rather than produce the image and discuss it as part of a group, such a practice would have had absolutely nothing to do with the original function of the text of *The Mystic Ark*.

Once it is realized that the purpose of the text of *The Mystic Ark* was to provide the information necessary for producing the image of the *Ark* and for a basic understanding of its imagery so that others could conduct discussions similar to those held by Hugh at Saint Victor, the relation of *The Mystic Ark* to the treatise of *The Moral Ark* becomes much easier to understand, as does the original sequence of texts at Saint Victor. The fact is, *The Moral Ark* is perfectly understandable without an image, and as much as 40 percent of the manuscripts of *The Moral Ark* appear alone, without being accompanied by the text of *The Mystic Ark*. In the original sequence of texts as represented by the manuscripts of Saint Victor and the *Indiculum, The Mystic Ark* did not come before *The Moral Ark* so that the reader could form a mental picture of *The Mystic Ark*. Not only is such a thing unnecessary for *The Moral Ark*; it would be confusing, since so much of the imagery in *The Mystic Ark* has little or nothing to do with *The Moral Ark*, while much of the discussion in *The Moral Ark* is not directly related to the image of *The Mystic Ark*. *The Mystic Ark* originally came before *The Moral Ark* because it was known at Saint Victor—whether Hugh was directly responsible for the establishment of the sequence in the manuscript tradition or not—that *The Moral Ark* came out of *The Mystic Ark*, that *The*

Moral Ark was a subset of *The Mystic Ark*. Thus, the purpose of the original sequence of texts at Saint Victor was first to present the basis of the entire *Ark* lectures, the image of *The Mystic Ark*, in *reportatio* form, and then to offer what Hugh's contemporary audience saw as the most original part of those lectures, *The Moral Ark*, as written by Hugh himself.

The original closing to *The Moral Ark* (*edificatam esse leteris*) is tied in with the original sequence of texts. Its point was not to "introduce" the painting of *The Mystic Ark*, properly speaking. It was, more precisely, to act as an encouragement to others to undertake discussions based upon the image of the *Ark*. When Hugh concludes by stating

> And, in fact, there is still more that I might have said if I were not afraid of wearying you. Therefore, let us now propose the exemplar of our Ark itself, as we have promised. This we have painted externally in order that you may learn from without what you ought to do within . . .

he is not exactly "introducing" an image of *The Mystic Ark* or even a written description of an image of *The Mystic Ark*. He is saying that *The Moral Ark* is only part of a broader subject that he now encourages his audience to enter into in its entirety: *The Mystic Ark*, something that they must undertake for themselves. The means of doing this, he states, is the painting that he himself made specifically for this purpose. Far from simply ending on a conventional note, *The Moral Ark* prompts its readers to initiate their own *Ark* discussions, having just had the most original part of the *Ark* lectures as an example of how the painting could act as the basis for these potentially wide-ranging discussions. This is the model of teaching "by word and example" (*docere verbo et exemplo*) that was the very basis of collegial spirituality, as articulated so well by Caroline Bynum.[194] It is also a perfect illustration of Peter of Celle's comment, made not long after Hugh had died, "If new things please you, look into the writings of Master Hugh."[195]

But if *The Mystic Ark* is not an "illustration" of *The Moral Ark*, and if *The Moral Ark* is not an "introduction" to *The Mystic Ark*, why do several passages appear in *The Moral Ark* that refer to the painting of *The Mystic Ark* without any obvious reason for doing so?[196] Although these passages have caused some confusion among scholars trying to come to terms with the relationship between the two texts, there is a straightforward explanation for such a seemingly odd conceit from a writer as aware and disciplined as Hugh. While the first and most important of these passages places the painting of *The Mystic Ark* in its larger cosmic context, a context that Hugh is thereafter free to more or less ignore, their common characteristic is that they all take for granted that the reader fully understands the role of these otherwise unexplained references to the painting. They do this, quite simply, because Hugh had reason to expect that his specialized audience—the small but vibrant world of highly educated and well-read canons and monks—would already know what the role of the painting in *The Moral Ark* was. It was said of Hugh's writings in general by Robert of Torigny, abbot of Mont-Saint-Michele, around thirteen years after his death, that they were so well known that it was unnecessary to even name them.[197] This would have been even more the case with the *Ark* texts in particular, especially around the time of their composition, because of their polemical aspect and unusual popularity. But the fact that there are eighty-eight known extant manuscript copies of *The Mystic Ark* tells us more than that it was extremely popular (sixty extant manuscript copies of any medieval text is considered to be evidence of an unusually high popularity[198]). The great effort and expense of producing texts in the Middle Ages had the attendant effect that copies of recent writings were typically acquired only when they were specifically desired, when their subject was already fairly well known. With most texts, such knowledge would have involved only an awareness of the subject matter of the writing in the narrow sense. The unique characteristic of the text of *The Mystic Ark*, however, is that it is based on an image, or, more precisely, that it is based on a series of lectures that was based on an image. Basic familiarity with it would necessarily imply an awareness of this unique aspect. Furthermore, it has been said that Hugh was the most renowned master in Paris after Abelard, and that, when Abelard was not in town, his lectures at Saint Victor probably attracted more students than those of any of the other masters.[199] Given that Abelard had left Paris to become abbot of Saint-Gildas around 1125 to 1127[200]—and given that the preface to *The Moral Ark* implies that the *Ark* lectures had created something of a sensation—it seems an unavoidable conclusion that those contemporaries of one of the two most popular teachers and the most famous theologian of his day who were acquiring manuscript copies of *The Mystic Ark* knew that it was not a literary work properly speaking, but a *reportatio* whose purpose was to act as a vehicle for undertaking discussions similar to Hugh's, based on the image of *The Mystic Ark*. Likewise, it seems that those acquiring copies of *The Moral Ark* early on equally knew that this work—of which there are no less than 143 known extant copies, making it one of Hugh's three most popular writings and comparable in popularity at the time to Bernard of Clairvaux's *Homilies on the Canticle of Canticles*[201]—came out of a lecture series based on a painting, a lecture series of which it was the most original part, as is clearly stated in its preface. This apparent awareness of the circumstances of the *Ark* lectures is why Hugh could refer in *The Moral Ark* to a painting that he had not really explained, that was not necessary to understand *The Moral Ark*, and that he most certainly did not expect his readers to know first from their having painted it. And it is why, at least in the beginning, that *The Mystic Ark* could be without proper title, preface, or section headings, and could still be placed before *The Moral Ark* without the expectation of confusion.

It is unclear exactly when, where, and why the original arrangement of the *Ark* texts was altered, though it seems to have been quite early. It may be that, once the two writings began to be disseminated beyond the immediate sphere of influence of Saint Victor, the less authoritative status and less traditional aspect of the *reportatio* of *The Mystic Ark* seemed to copyists to suggest this text as secondary to the phenomenally popular (and so, in a sense, authoritative) *The Moral Ark*. Even so, the general purpose of *The Mystic Ark* continued to be understood, as indicated by the various titles given to it by scribes. In any event, the sequence of the *Ark* texts and the closing of *The Moral Ark* no longer remained standard. The placement of *The Mystic Ark* after *The Moral Ark* and the use of a number of shorter closings (most notably *fastidium non timerem*) appear at first to have been attempts to avoid the perceived awkwardness of the original closing (*edificatam esse leteris*), which certainly might have given the appearance to some of bringing the book to a self-contradictory conclusion by introducing a painting that had already been mentioned as its basis (even though it actually prompted the reader to undertake his or her own painting and discussions). Although such an edit implies an effort at clarification, it also indicates, more significantly, a certain distance from the original conception as found at Saint Victor, where *The Mystic Ark* was first envisioned and first flourished. Whether this distance was one of time or location is impossible to say. Given the continued tradition of the original sequence and closing of *The Moral Ark* at Saint Victor into the thirteenth century, it seems that the altered sequence and closings were related to the use of outside copyists at first. But soon, it appears that many scribes simply copied whatever format was at hand, with no observable pattern between sequence and the various closings. Although the fact that there are so many permutations of sequence and closings shows that there was a fair amount of dissatisfaction with the inadequacies of the *reportatio* of *The Mystic Ark*, the same basic relationship between *The Mystic Ark* and *The Moral Ark* and the same basic function of the *reportatio* remained in effect. And this function was, as before, to undertake through the vehicle of the *reportatio* discussion of the broader subject of *The Mystic Ark*, of which *The Moral Ark* was the more original part, in the collegial tradition of teaching by word and example (*docere verbo et exemplo*).

2. WHETHER *THE MYSTIC ARK* WAS PAINTED AT SAINT VICTOR, THE QUESTION OF EKPHRASIS, AND WHETHER *THE MYSTIC ARK* WAS MEANT TO BE PAINTED BY OTHERS

So far, the vast majority of the confusion caused by the *Ark* texts as discussed here has been the result of problems inherent in the text of *The Mystic Ark*. But equally serious confusion has arisen over the very subject of that text: the painting of *The Mystic Ark*. The reason for this is that the painting described in the text is both so large and so detailed that some scholars believe that it never existed at all, while others think that, if it did, it existed only in a reduced state, or that it was rarely produced after the original painting of Saint Victor, despite the great popularity of the text.[202] At the same time, some authors have thought that it must have been a manuscript illumination, some that it was a large parchment wall-hanging (like a wall map), others that it was a wall or floor painting, and others still that it existed as an image only in the minds of the readers of the text.[203]

Without detailing every author who has written on the subject, let me just say that, again, it is Sicard who has thought the most about the problem and who tries to offer a solution that addresses the variety of issues involved. As he sees it, *The Mystic Ark* was painted by Hugh at Saint Victor, bit by bit, in front of his audience as the *Ark* lectures and discussions progressed. He thinks that the word *planities* in the opening passage of *The Mystic Ark* alludes to the actual material surface on which the *Ark* was painted at Saint Victor and—since this word often refers to a horizontal surface and, on occasion, to the surface of a sheet of parchment—that this surface was not a wall, but most likely a large parchment wall-hanging or a floor painting (though in a later study he describes it strictly as a floor painting). He also feels, however, that this is an image that was written more than it was depicted, that after the original painting at Saint Victor it functioned more as a "verbal image"—apparently because no examples of it have survived—and that the text of *The Mystic Ark* was originally meant to be read as a literary work.[204]

It is not an easy thing to show, with a reasonable degree of certainty from a set of general instructions written for an essentially anonymous audience, that a painting in fact once existed at the time and place of writing. But *The Mystic Ark* is not just a set of instructions: it is a *reportatio*, the worked-up record of an eyewitness, and the phrasing of certain of its passages confirms not just that they were made by direct observation, but that the painting of *The Mystic Ark* did in fact exist at Saint Victor. These passages are few and inadvertent, but they are no less convincing for being so. To take an example, the specification that the "icons" of the Patriarchs and Apostles be half-images is neither rhetorical nor part of the content of the painting (Fig. 5, no. 5, 6).[205] It is simply a detail made from direct observation for no apparent reason other than that the creator of *The Mystic Ark* had portrayed them that way (although he himself had his reasons) and the reporter duly recorded this fact in his generally dull and matter-of-fact text. The *reportatio* of *The Mystic Ark* shows a fairly strong pattern of this type of very specific but meaningless detail. In one place, the reporter writes that Spring (and so the other Seasons) be painted "from the hips up" (Fig. 9).[206] In another, he specifies that the Winds be depicted "as if plunging headlong downward and as if jutting forward from the shoulders" (Fig. 2, no. 8).[207] A bit further on, he notes that the principal Winds should be shown blowing a double-horn, with the subordinate Winds blowing single horns.[208] And elsewhere, he states that the Signs of the Zodiac be horizontal while the Months be vertical (Fig. 2, no. 6).[209] As before, none of these details have any rhetorical quality. But they all indicate that the reporter employed direct observation of an existing painting (though, as I have shown, he was not consistent in this as a working method) and was not recounting some aspect of the meaning of the image. In a somewhat different vein, the same might be said about the personal comment discussed above regarding the "extraordinary arrangement" of the east-west temporal-spatial progression—that it is an indication of the practice of direct observation of an extant painting, even if that observation was inconsistently realized.[210] Given the general absence of a literary quality in this *reportatio*, there can be no other explanation for such specific but otherwise meaningless observations on the part of the reporter. Nor can the sentence "Because of its more suitable form in the painting, I myself have shortened the length to around four times" be understood in any other way than as evidence that *The Mystic Ark* was in fact painted at Saint Victor.[211]

The image of *The Mystic Ark* that existed at Saint Victor was not painted bit by bit by Hugh as the lecture progressed, as Sicard maintains, although it does seem that it was painted by Hugh himself.[212] Not only would such a process have been far too time-consuming for the relatively short discussion periods of the *collationes* during which the *Ark* lectures were held; such a thing would have contributed absolutely nothing to the content of the lectures.[213] The process of producing the painting of *The Mystic Ark* is in no way a metaphor or outline of "the practice of some exercise" for the restoration of the soul to its creator, which was the subject of the *Ark* lectures and texts.[214] Such a restoration could only come from the internalization of the material presented in the painting, the logic of which does have a sequential component, but not that given in the *reportatio*. For example, in taking up the crucial four ascents of the Ark (Fig. 5, no. 7–10), the *reportatio* of *The Mystic Ark* does so by means of a sequence that is based on the convenience of verbal presentation, rather than through the sequences of spiritual ascent or descent, which are the only ones pertinent to their meaning and even their reason for being (cf. Fig. 8).[215] Nor does the treatise of *The Moral Ark* support the idea of the painting being made bit by bit during the lectures; it begins with the Majesty, although any production of *The Mystic Ark* must begin with the center point for simple compositional reasons—as the *reportatio* in fact does. Additional examples from both *Ark* texts could be listed endlessly. Aside from this, the complete pointlessness of making the participants observe the composition, the drawing, and then the painting of the structure and figures—not to mention the recording of the vast number of inscriptions—would unquestionably have broken up the momentum of the lectures to such a degree that they could not possibly have achieved the success that Hugh says they had and that the large number of extant manuscripts confirms. Finally, if *The Moral Ark* can be used as a witness to this particular question, Hugh first presented a finished painting to the participants, clearly stating that the point of presenting this "whole" painting was to aid the participants in understanding the "parts" of the forthcoming lectures.[216]

Is it possible to deduce the medium in which *The Mystic Ark* was painted at Saint Victor? Sicard is not wrong in suggesting that it might have been depicted on a wall-hanging or a floor; but the reasoning he uses to reach this view is wrong. The term *planities*, upon which he bases his opinion, can mean any surface, although in medieval texts it most commonly means a level stretch of ground, and in at least one source it refers to an open space in a church.[217] As I have shown above, however, *planities* also carries a geometrical sense that was extremely common in the school culture of the time and that Hugh uses frequently in his *Practica geometriae*. When the text states, "First, I find the center point on the surface (*planitie*) where I wish to depict the Ark . . . ," the tone is that of the schoolmaster working his way through a problem in geometry; the term *planities* here does not refer to the actual material surface on which the original *Ark* was painted at Saint Victor (Hugh uses the term *faciem membranae* to indicate a parchment surface elsewhere), but is simply a natural part of the technical vocabulary of the description of this geometric process.[218] The painting of *The Mystic Ark* could have been painted in a number of different media at Saint Victor, including as a wall or floor or even ceiling painting, as well as a wall-hanging.

A floor or ceiling painting, however, seems very unlikely, given the pedagogical nature of the *Ark*. As a floor painting, its composition is such that it would have been impossible for Hugh to conduct effective discussions without the participants standing on the painting itself to see the important details of the Ark proper—not something that is likely to have been planned for the original image. Nor does it seem probable that the *Ark* was painted on a ceiling, an arrangement that would have forced the audience to bend their heads back for extended periods of time, something that would hardly be conducive to conversation, especially the regular periods of conversation that are a part of the nature of the *Ark* discussions.

A parchment wall-hanging at Saint Victor also seems improbable, though for reasons related to size rather than use. The text of *The Mystic Ark* gives no instructions regarding the absolute size of the painting, only suggesting relative proportions for the Ark proper. Beyond this, everything else is left up to the person producing the image, whether medieval or modern. These proportions, however, in combination with a likely minimum size for the central cubit based on legibility of image and inscription, are all that are needed to produce the *Ark*—this apparently being just what the reporter had in mind. For example, I base my own production of the *Ark* on a central cubit that is one-half digit square, a minimal medieval unit of measurement that yields an Ark proper with a length of 100 digits (190 cm.; 6 ft. 3 in.), just large enough to be comfortably legible as a pedagogical work of art.[219] But my self-imposed rule of using historical models for the various components of the *Ark* (rather than simply drawing my own) and my overriding concern that the general composition be visually suitable for a wide variety of modern viewers have led me to be far more liberal in regard to the overall size of the work than might have been the case at Saint Victor.[220] Indeed, my studies have shown that the size of *The Mystic Ark* could have varied significantly from production to production. Even with a central cubit, Ark proper, and world (all of the components that carry small-scale detail) of the same size as that used in my arrangement, productions could range anywhere from approximately the size of the Ebstorf Map to somewhat larger, depending on the treatment by the individual artist of the remaining components of the air, ether, and Majesty (components for which, unlike the central cubit, Ark, and world, detail was not particularly crucial). The Ebstorf Map was the largest map to have survived into modern times (358 by 356 cm.; 11 ft. 9 in. by 11 ft. 8 in.).[221] A wall-hanging this size could be prohibitively expensive. For example, the cost of the late fourteenth-century Evesham Map (94 by 46 cm.; 3 ft. 1 in. by 1 ft. 6 in.) has been estimated as comparable to the annual earnings of an agricultural worker or the cost of a farm wagon and horse.[222] A wall-hanging of *The Mystic Ark* approximately the size of the Ebstorf Map (127,448 sq. cm.; 137.2 sq. ft.) would have around thirty times the area of the Evesham Map (4324 sq cm.; 4.65 sq. ft.), for which one would expect a commensurate increase in cost. Geography was an important part of medieval higher education in both its spiritual and its more narrowly geographic applications. The regular, long-term use of a world map as a standard part of the course of education at an institution with an active school could have been seen by many as justifying the expense of even a large example. While the painting of *The Mystic Ark* is a work that brought much of this learning together in a very effective manner, it was not itself a standard part of any course of learning. However popular the *Ark* was in the twelfth and succeeding centuries, it seems highly unlikely that the great expense of a wall-hanging of the *Ark* could have been justified at Saint Victor in the late 1120s, a time of both financial insecurity and enormous demands from a rapidly growing library.

It thus seems probable that *The Mystic Ark* as it existed at Saint Victor took the form of a wall painting, a relatively inexpensive medium. It is impossible to say where this wall painting was located at the abbey. But if the *Ark* lectures were given only to the brethren of the inner school, the painting of the *Ark* was most likely painted on one of the walls of the main cloister, though it could also have been on the walls of the parlor, the church, or some other claustral building. If the lectures were also given to the students of the outer school (about which we know next to nothing), as seems likely, the location of the painting would depend on whether these students were allowed into the claustrum of Saint Victor or, as was more traditional, they were excluded at this time. If they were excluded, then the wall painting of *The Mystic Ark* would have been located at some other place in the monastery accessible to both groups, something that might include any suitable interior or exterior wall outside the claustrum, including the church.

Some scholars have wondered whether Hugh originally intended that others should paint *The Mystic Ark* for themselves. Perhaps the best place to begin approaching this issue is with the question of whether *The Mystic Ark* was originally meant to be read as a literary work, that is, whether it was originally meant to be read primarily for its own sake by an individual and without the production of an image of *The Mystic Ark*.

It has been suggested by Evans, for example, that the text of *The Mystic Ark* is an extended work of "fictive painting." But *The Mystic Ark* is simply not in the genre of ekphrasis, the literary description of an imaginary work of art.[223] To begin with, to accept the evidence that *The Mystic Ark* is a *reportatio* is to preclude the idea that it is ekphrasis. But, aside from this, ekphrasis has, from Homer to Baudri de Bourgueil, a literary quality by definition of its very genre, something that is far, far absent from *The Mystic Ark*, where, for the most part, nothing more is found than a bare, utilitarian, and at times even hurried description. Hugh's *De vanitate mundi* is filled with instances of his ability to create verbal imagery that is extremely evocative, in the same way that good ekphrasis is evocative, conjuring up captivating and colorful images of pleasure craft at sea, desert caravans, idyllic manor life, wedding feasts, and even the idealism of learning.[224] Yet not a hint of this is found in *The Mystic Ark*. Indeed, the reason why Hugh tolerated such careless work in the first recension—and why so little effort was made toward clarity in the second—was that the text was not meant to be read for its own sake; what mattered were the oral discussions that followed the visual production of the *Ark*, something that would be unaffected by the poor style of the *reportatio*. This is why the text has none of the standard accompaniments of proper title, preface, and section headings, but still remained highly popular. It would be a very insipid example of ekphrasis indeed that lifts passages from Bede, from one of Hugh's other works, and perhaps from Isidore—and typically very common passages, literarily, at that. It is hardly ekphrasis that makes entirely mundane references to Hugh's other writings or that, after giving a description of the image, has a separate section for inscriptions. And it is not ekphrasis at all that announces at one point, after one hopelessly garbled passage and before another wholeheartedly mechanical one, "In all of these, we will refrain from much discussion because of the abbreviated nature of this work."[225]

Nor was *The Mystic Ark* originally primarily meant to be read as a literarily simpler form than ekphrasis, as a text primarily written for either individual memorization and/or meditation.[226] It is not a text that lends itself in any way either to reading or to the creation of an image of *The Mystic Ark* in the mind of the reader with any facility. In one place, the reporter lists a number of entirely unrelated miscellaneous elements of *The Mystic Ark* as a group, without any concern whatsoever for either compositional or conceptual integration into the overall structure of *The Mystic Ark*. In another, a very long list of inscriptions is given that is based on a logic of description, not the logic of the concept of *The Mystic Ark*. In another still, concern for the real-world practicalities of the proportions of the Ark take precedence over the unique ability of the mind to ignore such mundane realities in the creation of mental images—something that also contradicts the claim of ekphrasis.[227] Here, the textually minor reference to the color segments of the four ascents contradicts their conceptually prominent role in the seminar context.[228] And there, neither the idea of the four different Arks nor the works of creation and of restoration are ever explicitly discussed, despite their absolute centrality to the concept of *The Mystic Ark*—not for any rhetorical reasons, but because the text is an outline of sorts of certain information, not a comprehensive account, as will soon be discussed. But perhaps the most obvious argument against the idea that *The Mystic Ark* was primarily meant to be read is that the unavoidable sequence of internalizing information that constitutes the process of reading is contrary to Hugh's own characterization of the *Ark*, that one should view the whole first before attempting to understand the parts[229]—not to mention the fact that if the text were meant to be read, one would expect that Hugh himself would have written it. While I agree with Mary Carruthers that *The Mystic Ark* could have served as an "elementary" memory diagram in some way, the evidence indicates that this would have been only a secondary function; in my opinion, its primary function was precisely as described by Hugh himself in *The Moral Ark*: group discussions.

Although *The Mystic Ark* was written for outside use—and not for the auditors of the original lecture and discussion group at Saint Victor, as Sicard inexplicably believes, apparently misunderstanding the traditional justification for writing that is found in the preface to *The Moral Ark*[230]—it is impossible to say whether the image of *The Mystic Ark* was actually made elsewhere, outside of Saint Victor. However, the text was laboriously copied over and over again for a reason. The same passages that show that the *reportatio* of *The Mystic Ark* was originally not meant to be read primarily as a literary work serve equally to indicate that it was originally intended to aid others in undertaking their own painting. It would be redundant to go over all these points again, as it would be to draw attention once more to the original conclusion of *The Moral Ark* that prompts readers to enter into their own discussions based on the painting. That no examples of a painting of *The Mystic Ark* survive from outside Saint Victor in no way bears upon Hugh's intent in the matter. But the great popularity of the text of *The Mystic Ark* strongly suggests that it was in fact made elsewhere, and probably often—this is the only function of the much copied *reportatio*—something confirmed by any number of informal titles, given by copyists, that refer to the action of painting the *Ark*; for example, the very precise title of one twelfth-century manuscript: *How It [the Ark] Ought to Be Painted.*[231]

As a pedagogical image intended for lecture and group discussions particularly among communities of canons and monks, it seems likely that later productions of *The Mystic Ark* were made in the same physical setting that Saint Victor's painting was: the cloister or lecture hall. In either case, as the focus of group discussions, the image of *The Mystic Ark* was not public art; it was in all likelihood not expected to be on permanent display; and thus it would not necessarily have been subject to the material standards of large-scale public art. It certainly could have been made in any medium, though one would expect that the less expensive medium of wall painting that was probably used at Saint Victor would be the most likely choice elsewhere as well. At the same time, I suspect that there were often sketchier versions than Hugh's own *Ark*, which he describes as a proper work of art, versions that were not fully finished and that were never intended to be preserved. Only a professional artist or someone following in the tradition of the monastic artist, as Hugh himself seems to have, could have produced the *Ark* at the level described by Hugh in *The Moral Ark*.[232] And a professional lay artist could not, in all likelihood, have reproduced the *Ark* without constant supervision by an educated canon regular, monk, or member of the schools, as my own efforts at producing the *Ark* through the efforts of a skilled digital artist have made only too clear. Furthermore, the production of images on the basis of the second recension—the more widely distributed of the two recensions—would have been further complicated by that text's uncomprehending elimination of the altered proportions of the Ark.[233] What all of these images would have had in common—the painting at Saint Victor, which certainly seems to have existed, and images of whatever sort at institutions elsewhere, which seem likely—is a large-scale format. I say this for two reasons. First, the large size is absolutely necessary to incorporate the detail and inscriptions of the *Ark*—something that a manuscript illumination, which one would expect to be part of any process of individual reading, could not do. Second, the large-scale format comes right out of its traditional function as a pedagogical image whose context was one of communal discussions, whether by canons, monks, or advanced students, something that is the subject of the next section.

3. HOW THE TEXT OF *THE MYSTIC ARK* WAS MEANT TO BE UNDERSTOOD AS A SET OF INSTRUCTIONS

To the degree that the evidence allows, I have shown that *The Mystic Ark* was originally not primarily intended to be read by an individual as a literary work, and that it was meant to be produced by others outside of Saint Victor. It is a corollary of this that *The Mystic Ark* was meant to be produced for group lecture and discussions. While this may not be an unusually controversial statement to make in itself, an understanding of this issue is intimately bound up with the erroneous idea, assumed by so many scholars, that the text of *The Mystic Ark* is a detailed set of "step-by-step" instructions describing the process of drawing and painting the image of *The Mystic Ark*.[234]

This confusion comes about from *The Mystic Ark* being structured in the semblance, not the actuality, of step-by-step directions. This semblance does not properly recognize standard artistic procedure.

In an actual step-by-step process, the person producing *The Mystic Ark* would typically first lay out the general composition entirely. He or she would begin by finding (locating) the center point upon which the entire image is to be centered, something that assumes a fairly exact sense of how large the image will be when fully composed (Fig. 5, no. 1). Then the central cubit, which determines the general size of the Ark proper and so of the entire image, would be constructed around the center point. This would be followed by the construction of the first stage (Fig. 4), which would be determined on the basis of the cubit-module of the central cubit. At this point, major components either inside or outside of the Ark proper could be laid out. If the person chose to do those inside, he or she would construct the second and third stages, which are dependent for their construction upon the first stage (Fig. 4). After the remaining components of the Ark proper were laid out, the major compositional component of the earth would be drawn (dependent for its construction upon the Ark), followed by the major compositional components of the quaternary harmony (dependent upon the earth), the air (dependent upon the quaternary harmony), and the ether (dependent upon the air) (Fig. 2, no. 9, Fig. 4). Although figure drawing could, in principle, be done for one major component before the construction of the next, common medieval practice was to lay out the general structure of the entire composition first. Thus, the next step would be the laying out of the final major component of the composition of the *Ark*, the Majesty and seraphim, which would finalize the overall size and composition of the image (Fig. 2, no. 1, 3). This would be followed by figure drawing, properly speaking, and various detail work; gilding (e.g., the cross of the central cubit); and then the painting process. Finally, the inscriptions would be added, though some might have been done earlier, depending on the precise requirements of the individual components.[235]

This, however, is not the process given in the *reportatio* of *The Mystic Ark*. While *The Mystic Ark* simulates the general order of a step-by-step method—center point, first stage, remaining stages, other components of the Ark, earth, air, ether, Majesty—a logical artistic process is not actually followed. For example, after finding the center point, the reporter describes the production of the central cubit, the component that immediately surrounds the center point. The first major component to be taken up in the text, the reporter describes it as if its figure of the Lamb of God were to be immediately drawn and as if the cubit were to be immediately gilded and painted. He says this despite common artistic practice that calls for the production of the general composition first, and despite the fact that the rest of the entire compositional structure is to be constructed around the cubit whose center point would continue to be used for a great deal of work with compass and straightedge, work that would ruin the gilding and painting of the central cubit. Furthermore, while the reporter mentions only colors that are important symbolically to the meaning of *The Mystic Ark*, the same semblance of painting each component as soon as it is drawn is continued throughout the text; this, too, is contrary to contemporary artistic practice, in which the artist would normally apply one color at a time to the entire image, rather than painting each component individually.[236]

Never intending that the *reportatio* should be understood as actual artistic practice, the reporter—who was clearly not an artist—instead simply attempts to provide a component-by-component description of *The Mystic Ark* in the simplest and most complete way that he can. This is the key to understanding the original function of the text of *The Mystic Ark*. For within this component-by-component structure is an accompanying sequence of interpretations; the basic meaning of each component is typically given (at least in the first two of the three unintentionally different sections discussed above), but the relation of a given component in regard to the larger image of *The Mystic Ark* normally is not. For example, the discussion of the broader significance of the central cubit is in part unclear because certain of the interpretations dependent on the specific imagery of the cubit are given before the complete context of the cubit has been described—a situation that arises because of the reporter's chosen method of attempting to present structure and meaning at the same time. Thus, the reporter's goal is neither to provide an actual step-by-step set of instructions for producing *The Mystic Ark* nor to give a synthetic interpretation of the *Ark*. What he is trying to do is to provide an outline of the basic information necessary for others to enter into their own relatively independent lectures and discussions, as had been done at Saint Victor, and without any attempt at imposing a structure for these discussions through the arrangement of the *reportatio*. Toward this end, a certain amount of interpretation is given in the text, and there is even the occasional trace of passages with a sermon-like tone, perhaps vestiges of the original lectures by way of the reporter's personal notes, some possibly revised by Hugh.[237] But, ultimately, this presentation is irregular and the whole must be, to whatever degree, synthesized and articulated by the person leading the discussions, undoubtedly with the original intention that the participants should fully join in, both of these factors being something that would add a dimension of varied meaning to *The Mystic Ark*. It is in this context of communal discussions that Hugh describes the origin of *The Mystic Ark* lectures, and how he presents the role of the painting of the Ark within those lectures.[238]

Chapter Four

CONCLUSIONS

And so we see why *The Mystic Ark*, a text traditionally ascribed to Hugh of Saint Victor, a scholar renowned for his clarity and order, could be so unclear and disorderly: because it was not actually written by Hugh himself but by an anonymous student reporter, although Hugh very much remains its author, morally speaking. Not a finely polished *reportatio* of the sort described by Laurence of Westminster, the *reportatio* process employed by the reporter was flawed, with Hugh's participation being limited and irregular. The result was a very careless text, one that is at times unclear, confused, and inconsistent. Its writer, on occasion, gets ahead of himself, displays a weak knowledge of the Bible, exhibits a fundamental lack of connection with the basic logic of the structure of *The Mystic Ark*, and turns to outside sources (sometimes unclearly and even incorrectly used), as well as to writings by Hugh, because of a lack of full understanding of his subject.

Hugh's conception of *The Mystic Ark* did not change in any significant way during the course of the *Ark* lectures. *The Moral Ark* does not represent the original state of the painting of *The Mystic Ark*, nor does the text of *The Mystic Ark* embody a later, more complete conception of *The Mystic Ark* than that found in *The Moral Ark*. *The Moral Ark* is a subset of the broader *Ark* lectures, the part that was seen by contemporaries as the most original, and in no way presents a complete view of those lectures or even of the concept of *The Mystic Ark*. Along these lines, the crucial components of the three periods and the cosmos were present in the original painting.

Similarly, there was no change of conception between the first and second recensions of *The Mystic Ark*, and neither recension was made by Hugh personally. It seems that the inherently more authoritative first recension, by the student reporter, was retained by the in-house scriptorium of Saint Victor for its own use and for that of very closely related individuals and institutions. The second recension is a very poor attempt at clarification of the careless work of the first, and appears to have been made by an external commercial scribe because of other demands on the internal scriptorium. This recension seems to have often been used when requests for copies of *The Mystic Ark* were made by people and institutions other than those with unusually close ties to Saint Victor.

Until more convincing arguments are made, the most specific we can be about the date of the painting of *The Mystic Ark*, the *Ark* lectures, *The Moral Ark*, and the first recension of the *reportatio* of *The Mystic Ark* is that they all stem sometime from 1125 to early 1130, each appearing or taking place in the order just given. Likewise, until more compelling reasoning is given, the evidence as it now stands suggests that the second recension of *The Mystic Ark* was probably made sometime after Hugh's death in early 1141.

Neither the text nor the painting of *The Mystic Ark* is an "illustration" of *The Moral Ark*, nor is *The Moral Ark* an "introduction" to the text or painting of *The Mystic Ark. The Mystic Ark* was never originally intended as an "appendix" to *The Moral Ark.* It was not originally meant to be read primarily as a literary work, whether as ekphrasis or in a rhetorically simpler way. If the text of *The Mystic Ark* was used as a memory aid, this was only a secondary function: its primary function was to act as the basis for group discussions, as explicitly described in *The Moral Ark.* At least in the very beginning, it could be expected that those who asked for copies of *The Mystic Ark* knew that it was a *reportatio* for producing the image of *The Mystic Ark* and understood its relation to *The Moral Ark.*

A painting of *The Mystic Ark* existed at Saint Victor, probably as a wall painting and probably by Hugh himself. It was not painted bit by bit, before the audience, as the lecture progressed. Hugh originally intended that *The Mystic Ark* be painted by others, outside of Saint Victor; his concern in the writing of the Ark texts was not primarily with the original auditors of the *Ark* lectures. Although the great popularity of *The Mystic Ark* suggests that it was made elsewhere, it is impossible to confirm such a thing, since *The Mystic Ark* was not public art; it was a pedagogical image. These assumed images were in all likelihood not up to the material standards of public art or to those of the original painting of Saint Victor, which was a proper work of art, according to Hugh.

The text of *The Mystic Ark* is not meant to act as an actual "step-by-step" set of instructions describing the artistic process of creating a painting of *The Mystic Ark.* Its purpose is to aid others in undertaking, in a relatively independent way, a series of lectures and discussions similar to those conducted at Saint Victor under Hugh, the focus of which is the pedagogical image of *The Mystic Ark*. It does this by presenting an outline of the imagery in a component-by-component fashion, accompanied by interpretations for most (though not all) of the imagery, interpretations that are typically limited to the specific imagery involved and unrelated to *The Mystic Ark* as a whole. A certain amount of this interpretation of the whole was apparently intended to be generated by the participants, something that would add a potential constant of anywhere from slightly to moderately variant readings to the conceptual dynamic of *The Mystic Ark*.

And so, in coming to terms with the previous literature on the painting and *reportatio* of *The Mystic Ark*, the "difficulty of these things" has hardly been less than it must have been for poor Lucilius so long ago. But we see that, once the unnecessary verbal contortions are done away with, the origins of the image and text are really quite simple, as is their relation to the *Ark* lectures and the treatise of *The Moral Ark*. The result is a far better understanding of an amazingly popular image and text that, together, form one of the most important sources we have for medieval art history, and of the striking pedagogical role that a complex image could play in the spiritual and intellectual controversies of the day.

NOTES

1. On the origin of Hugh, see Croydon (1939); Taylor (1957); Javelet (1960); Mietke (1972); Poirel (1998:11–12, 30–32; 1998b:192). On Hugh and Saint Victor in general, Bonnard (1904), Châtillon (1952:147–162), Bautier (1991), Sicard (1991), and, with special reference to reform, Bautier (1981). On Hugh's reputation during the Middle Ages, see Richard of Saint Victor, *Benjamin Maior* 1:4, *PL* 196:67, cited in Häring (1982:192). For Hugh as a second Augustine, see Anonymus Carthusiensis, *De religionum origine* 24, col. 55; and *Veterum scriptorum testimonia, PL* 175: CLXVI. For a short bibliography on the influence of Augustine in the works of Hugh, see Zinn (1975:62, n. 5).
2. Rudolph (1990:32–47), Gasparri (1996:xxxiii–xxxv, xxxviii–xxxix; 2001), Poirel (2001).
3. This will be taken up more fully in my forthcoming book on the *Ark*, but is described in large part in Rudolph (1999:21–29).
4. Sicard (1991:31; 1993:96–97, 99; 2001:10*; cf. 2001:29*–62*).
5. Seneca, *Ep*. 58:20, v.1:157.
6. Rudolph (1990:32–47).
7. Sicard (1991, 1993). See also Smalley (1952:95–97), Baron (1957:182–185), Van den Eynde (1960:69–83), Squire (1962), del Basso (1965), Zinn (1968, 1971), Bronder (1972), Ehlers (1972), Ohly (1972), Zinn (1972, 1974, 1975), Obrist (1986), Lecoq (1989), Skubiszewski (1990:265–267) (my thanks to Professor Skubiszewski for providing me with a copy of this article), Carruthers (1992:42–45, 123, 231–239, 253), McGinn (1992:v.2:376–387), Zinn (1992), Evans (1994), Carruthers (1998:243–246), Poirel (1998: 129–132), Sicard (2001), and Carruthers and Weiss (2002). An English translation of *The Mystic Ark* by Jessica Weiss follows Carruthers and Weiss (2002). My own translation with extensive commentary will appear in my forthcoming study of *The Mystic Ark.*
8. Sicard does take up the question of whether *The Moral Ark* is a *reportatio*, seeing in it traces of orality, but concluding that it is not one (Sicard 1993: 21–26).
9. On the consistency of Hugh's thought, see McGinn (1992:v.2:374).
10. Hamesse (1988:83–87). I take the word "reporter" from the medieval term *reportator*; cf. Hamesse (1988:85).
11. Smalley (1952:201–202, 205).
12. Bischoff (1935), Weisweiler (1949:256–266), Croydon (1950), Smalley (1952:202), and Piazzoni (1982:862–865).
13. Laurence, *Ep*., pp. 912–913.

14. Hugh, *Descriptio mappe mundi*, prologue, p. 133; Gautier Dalché (1988: 54–55). On the literary style of Hugh, see Baron (1963:91–120).
15. Baron (1955:15).
16. The practice of making compilations of one kind or another of Hugh's teaching seems to have been common among his students. Hugh's *Notulae* were collected by his students from his lectures (Pollitt 1966:8–9). His *Miscellanea* seem to be a collection of extracts made by his students from his biblical commentaries (Lottin 1958:279–281).
17. This lack of clarity is a constant in Sicard's discussion of the two recensions of *The Mystic Ark* (Sicard 1993:73–99). See also Wirth (1999:386).
18. Hugh, *Mystic Ark* I, p. 123. "Que quadratura sexies tam longa sit quam lata . . . Ego tamen propter competentiorem formam in pictura usque ad quadruplam fere longitudinem breuiaui" (Gen. 6:15).
19. Hugh, *Mystic Ark* I, p. 123, ". . . et ita duas alias quadraturas sexies similiter longas ad latitudinem suam efficio."
20. Hugh, *Moral Ark* I:IV, I:V, II:I, pp. 20, 23–24, 26, 34; *Mystic Ark* IV, p. 139.
21. Hugh, *Mystic Ark* IX, XI, pp. 155, 157, and cf. X, p. 156.
22. Hugh, *Mystic Ark* IV–VI, pp. 140–151, esp. IV, pp. 145, 146–147.
23. Hugh, *Mystic Ark* IV, p. 140.
24. Hugh, *Mystic Ark* XI, pp. 157–158. Cf. Isidore, *De natura rerum* 11:3, p. 217, where the table begins with fire, and so one might expect the *rota* to have fire at the top, as it does in Paris BN 5543:136 (Fig. 10). The potential influence of a literary source has also been commented upon by Sicard (1993:60–63, 85), though with different conclusions, as discussed below. But in this immediate regard, Sicard suggests that Hugh was looking at Bede's *De temporum ratione* 35, making reference to the schema from the *Patrologia Latina* edition (*PL* 90:461–462). The text of *The Mystic Ark*, however, is less well coordinated with Bede's presentation than it is with Isidore's. Although the schema tradition for either Isidore or Bede could well have served as a model for the reporter, this is only because the passage from Bede was originally unillustrated, the schema commonly found illustrating this passage typically being introduced from Isidore by copyists (cf. Edson 1998:66), something that is the case with the *PL* schema, whose inscription suggests such a transference.
25. Hugh, *Mystic Ark* IV–VI, pp. 140–151, esp. 146:187 (*scalam* for ascent), 146:188 (*scala* for ladder), 146:190 (*scala* for ladder), 146:191 (*scala* for ladder), 146:192 (*scale* for ascents), 146:193 (*scala* for ascent), 146:194 (*scala* for ladder), 148:235–236 (*ascension* for ascent), 151:21 (*ascensus* for ascent). This is separate from the reporter's earlier practice of calling the same elements "beams" (*tigna*) when they are conceived of as components of the naval architecture of the *Ark*.
26. Hugh, *Mystic Ark* VI, p. 151.
27. Hugh, *Mystic Ark* IV, p. 147. Cf. the school text of the *Didascalicon* 4:6, p. 76, where Hugh makes the distinction between the Evangelists and their

symbols as a matter of course. On *The Mystic Ark* as being conceived for a school context, see the comments of Green (1943:485) on the *Indiculum*.

28. Hugh, *Mystic Ark* IV, pp. 142–146; the omission is from the third ladder of the Cold of the East (p. 142). Because the first two ladders of the ascent of the Cold of the East have colored divisions of three, I have assumed that the third ladder would as well in my production.
29. Hugh, *Mystic Ark, passim*, but for a few of many examples, see I, pp. 125–126 (Tree of Life, Book of Life); IV, pp. 140–141 (the names and characterizations of the four corners of the *Ark*); VII, p. 152 (Ox, Ass, Noah, Ham); XI, pp. 157–158 (components of the harmony).
30. Hugh, *Mystic Ark* XI, p. 159.
31. Hugh, *Mystic Ark* IX, p. 155.
32. Hugh, *Mystic Ark* II, pp. 131–132.
33. Hugh, *Mystic Ark* IV, p. 146. The order is correctly given in *Mystic Ark* IV, p. 142. Cf. Hugh, *Moral Ark* IV:IX, p. 113; *Didascalicon* 5:2, 6:2–6:5, pp. 96, 113–123; *De scriptures* 4, *PL* 175:12; *De tribus maximis*, p. 491; *De sacramentis* 1, prol. 4, *PL* 176:184–185. Bonaventure, *De reductione atrium* 5, p. 321.
34. Hugh, *Mystic Ark, passim*; for the specific passage under discussion, *Mystic Ark* IV, p. 139. See also Carruthers (1992:234 n. 39) and Sicard (1993:52 n. 85, 60, n. 102).
35. Hugh, *De tribus maximis*, p. 490. On this passage, see Carruthers (1992:233–234).
36. Hugh, *Mystic Ark* III, XI, pp. 132–138 (esp. 137–138), 157; cf. the "principal" passages on the *mappa mundi, Mystic Ark* XI, pp. 157, 161.
37. Hugh, *Mystic Ark* IV, pp. 142–143, 146.
38. Hugh, *Mystic Ark* II, p. 129. Some medieval scribes corrected this mistake, as does the *PL* edition. "Magister Hugo de Sancto Victore in scientia scripturarum nulli secundus in orbe . . . ," from Paris, BN lat. 15009:77r–77v, cited by Dickinson (1950:284–285).
39. Hugh, *Mystic Ark* I–IV (first section), IV–X (second section), XI (third section), pp. 121–140, 140–156, 157–162.
40. Hugh, *Mystic Ark* I, pp. 121–124.
41. For example, Hugh, *Mystic Ark* I, pp. 123–124.
42. Hugh, *Mystic Ark* I, pp. 123–125, esp. p. 123.
43. For another view of this problem, see Sicard (1993:76).
44. Hugh, *Mystic Ark* II, pp. 131–132. Sicard cites Rabanus Maurus as the source for this in the critical edition, but Rabanus was himself following the presentation in Bede, of which the *Ark* passage is a reduced version; cf. *passim*, but esp. the description of the sixth age: "Sexta etas, que nunc agitur, nulla annorum serie certa, sed ut etas decrepita ipsa morte totius seculi consumenda. Has erumpnosas planasque laboribus mundi etates quicunque felici morte uicerunt, septima iam sabbati perennis etate suscepti, octauam beate resurrectionis etatem, in qua cum Domino perhenniter

regnabunt, expectant." Bede, *De temporum ratione* 66, p. 464, "Sexta, que nunc agitur aetas, nulla generationum vel temporum serie certa, sed ut aetas decrepita ipsa totius saeculi morte consummanda. Has erumnosas plenasque laboribus mundi aetates quique felici morte vicerunt; septima iam sabbati perennis aetate suscepti, octavam beatae resurrectionis aetatem, in qua semper cum Domino regnent, exspectant." Bede follows Augustine, *De civitate Dei* 22:30, pp. 865–866. The reporter uses *diluuium*, as Augustine does, instead of Bede's *Noe*, as followed by Hugh in *Miscellanea* 1:82, *PL* 177:517. Cf. also, Bede, *De temporibus* 16, pp. 600–601.

45. Hugh, *Mystic Ark* I, pp. 125–126.
46. Hugh, *Mystic Ark* III, pp. 132–138; Sicard (1993:64).
47. Hugh, *Mystic Ark* III, p. 132 (lines 1–19, first passage), 132–137 (lines 20–131, second passage), 137–138 (lines 132–161, third passage).
48. Hugh, *De sacramentis*, pref., *PL* 176:173–174. *Dictassem*, which I translate as "written," could also mean "dictated."
49. For other examples of this practice with Hugh, which is widely recognized, see Van den Eynde (1960:75).
50. See Hugh, *Mystic Ark* VIII, p. 153, for passages copied from *Moral Ark* II:II–III, pp. 36–38.
51. Sicard (1993:64).
52. Bernard of Clairvaux, *Ep.* 77, v.7:184–200. Hugh incorporates part of Bernard's letter into his *De sacramentis*; cf. Bernard of Clairvaux, *Ep.* 77:11–15, v.7:193–196, and Hugh, *De sacramentis* 1:10:6–7 (*passim*), *PL* 176:335–341, which deals with the question of salvation before the period of grace, a subject directly related to Hugh's theme of the three periods of the history of salvation. On this subject, see esp. Feiss (1994) and, more broadly, Chenu (1968:172–173) and Luscombe (1969:186).
53. Hugh, *Mystic Ark* IV–X, pp. 140–156.
54. Hugh, *Moral Ark* II:II–III, pp. 36–38.
55. Hugh, *Mystic Ark* VIII, p. 153. A second direct dependency on *The Moral Ark* appears in the discussion of the lesser stages (*mansiunculae*); cf. Hugh, *Moral Ark* I:IV, p. 20 (*integro permanente intrinsecus*), and *Mystic Ark* IX, p. 154 (*intrinsecus integro permanente*).
56. Hugh, *Mystic Ark* XI, pp. 157–162.
57. The closing, "May God be blessed through all eternity," is a common, standard closing—one, however, that is not characteristic of Hugh's writings, properly speaking, though this type of closing is found from time to time in the sermons attributed to Hugh, sermons whose actual authorship is still being worked out. Cf. Van den Eynde (1960:33–34) and Schneyer (1964).
58. Hugh, *Moral Ark* IX, pp. 111–113. Cf. Schneider (1933:90–101), Ehlers (1973:120–135), Lecoq (1989:19–20, 22), and Sicard (1991:136).
59. Hugh, *Mystic Ark* XI, p. 157.
60. Hugh, *Mystic Ark* XI, pp. 158–159; this is discussed at greater length below, pp. 73–74.

61. Evans (1994:76–77).
62. Hugh, *Mystic Ark* I, p. 121. Cf. Hugh, *Practica geometriae* 7, 10, 15, 21, 22, 36, 37, pp. 22, 25, 30, 34, 35, 47, 48.
63. Macrobius, *Commentarii* 1:5:9, cf. 1:6:35, pp. 16, 24. Hugh, *Practica geometriae* 40, 41, 45, 48, 57, pp. 51, 53, 56, 60, 64. Vitruvius, *De architectura* 1:6:12, v.1:39. Hugh, *Didascalicon* 3:2, p. 50.
64. Macrobius, *Commentarii* 2:5:7–16, 2:7:9, pp. 111–112, 118–119.
65. Hugh, *Mystic Ark* I, II, pp. 123–125, 127, 130.
66. Macrobius (*Commentarii* 2:5–2:6, pp. 110–117) discusses Virgil (*Georgics* 1, lines 233–239, p. xxvi [sic]). Cf. also the following, all widely read: Ovid, *Metamorphoses* 1:46–51, v.1:20–21; Pliny, *Naturalis historiae* 2:68, v. 1:192; Martianus Capella, *De nuptiis* 6:602, p. 211; Isidore of Seville, *Etymologiae* 3:44, 13:6 (no pagination), and *De natura rerum* 10, pp. 209–213 (where he misunderstands, though cites, Virgil); and Bede, *De temporum ratione* 34, pp. 386–387.
67. On the belt of the zodiac as a *zona*, as seen in Fig. 12, see Vitruvius, *De architectura* 9:1:3, v.9:10.
68. Honorius Augustodunensis, *De imagine mundi* 1:39, PL 172:133, "Oceanus dicitur, quasi ocior annis, vel quasi zonarum limbus. Quinque enim zonas mundi in modum limbi ambit." Hugh, *Mystic Ark* I, pp. 121, 123, 124.
69. Hugh, *Mystic Ark* IV, pp. 138–139. Cf. Hugh, *Moral Ark* II:VI, p. 42.
70. For two widely read biblical references, cf. Ex. 27:2 and Lev. 4:7.
71. Only Squire (1962:63 n. 3) and Evans (1994:79) think that *The Moral Ark* refers to an image other than that described in *The Mystic Ark*. All other scholars are agreed that the two writings refer to the same image. For explicit discussions of Squire's position, see Zinn (1972:322, n. 14) and Sicard (1993:37).
72. Van den Eynde (1960); for the discussion here, see esp. pp. 69–83, 132–137.
73. Van den Eynde (1960:72).
74. Van den Eynde (1960:80–83). For the discussion above, see pp. 24–26.
75. Van den Eynde (1960:80).
76. Sicard (1993:119–138).
77. Sicard (1993:64–65).
78. See above, pp. 24–26.
79. Hugh, *Moral Ark* I:V, p. 23: "Trecentorum cubitorum longitudo presens seculum designat, quod tribus temporibus decurrit (id est tempore naturalis legis, tempore scripte legis, tempore gratie)."
80. Hugh, *Moral Ark* I:V, pp. 24–26: ". . . sancta Ecclesia, que ab initio mundi cepit, in tempore gratie per immolationem Agni immaculati redemptionem accepit . . . Ecclesia, que ab initio seculi fuit, in fine seculi redempta est." This passage is more easily understood in the context of Augustine's exegesis on the Ark, a knowledge of which it presupposes; cf. *Contra Faustum* 12:18, pp. 346–347.

81. Hugh, *Mystic Ark* I, pp. 124–125.
82. This is a simplification; these elements will be taken up in greater detail in my forthcoming study of the image of the *Ark*.
83. Hugh, *Moral Ark* IV:IX, p. 114 (horizontal); IV:IX, p. 115 (vertical): "prima mansio est natura, secunda mansio est lex scripta, tertia mansio est gratia"; cf. *Mystic Ark* IV, p. 139 (vertical): "in capite ascribo 'nature'; interiori autem superpono 'legis'; medie uero 'gratie'."
84. Hugh sees observance of the written law as beginning with Abraham, not Moses; *De sacramentis* 1:12:1–3, *PL* 176:347–351.
85. Hugh, *Moral Ark* II:XV, p. 53 (Paradise); IV:IV, IV:IX, pp. 95, 112 (journey of the Chosen People); II:VII, p. 44 (Twelve Tribes); IV:IX, pp. 111–112 (east-west progression).
86. Sicard (1991:29–30; 1993:57–67; 2001:9*).
87. Sicard (1991:29–30; 1993:62, 67).
88. Hugh, *Moral Ark* IV:I, IV:VII, pp. 87, 102; *Mystic Ark* XI, p. 160; *De tribus diebus* 4, p. 60; *De sacramentis* 1:1:24, *PL* 176:202. On this term as meaning the structure of the cosmos, see below, p. 94, n. 98.
89. Hugh, *Moral Ark* II:I, p. 34.
90. Hugh, *Moral Ark* I:II, I:V, pp. 17, 23–32.
91. Hugh, *Moral Ark* II:VI–VII, p. 42.
92. Hugh, *Moral Ark* IV:II, pp. 90–91.
93. Hugh, *Moral Ark* IV:IX, pp. 112–113.
94. Hugh, *Moral Ark* IV:IX, pp. 115–116.
95. Sicard (1993:60–62, 67, 85). For the discussion above, see pp. 16–18.
96. Hugh, *Moral Ark* II:II–III, pp. 36–38; cf. *Mystic Ark* VIII, p. 153. Discussed above, pp. 26–27.
97. Hugh, *Moral Ark* IV:V, p. 101 (six days); I:V, II:III, pp. 29–30, 37–38 (four elements). On the relation of the six days and the four elements, cf. Hugh, *Adnotationes in Pentateuchon* 4–6, *PL* 175:33–35; *Dialogus*, *PL* 176:17, 20; *De tribus maximis*, p. 491 (the preface to the *Chronicon*); *Chronicon* (as in Paris, BnF lat. 15009:3v, Green 1943, plate A); *De sacramentis* 1 prol. 2, 1:1:1–6, 1:1:24–25, 1:1:29, *PL* 176:183–184, 187–192, 202–203, 204.
98. Hugh, *Moral Ark* IV:IX, p. 116: "Ibi quoddam uniuersitatis corpus effingitur, et concordia singulorum explicatur." On *uniuersitatis corpus* as meaning the structure of the cosmos, cf. Plato (trans. Chalcidius), *Timaeus* 32A, p. 24 (*corpus universae*). On *concordia singulorum*, note the similarity of language in Ambrose, *Hexameron* 3:18, pp. 71–72; and Isidore of Seville, *De natura rerum* 11:2–3, pp. 215–217.
99. Hugh, *Mystic Ark* XI, p. 160 (*machina uniuersitatis*); XI, pp. 157–158. In my forthcoming book, I discuss why I believe the four elements were a part of the quaternary harmony. Byrhtferth's structure of the cosmos is virtually identical to that of *The Mystic Ark*, except for its nonstandard arrangement of the seasons and elements (for an excellent color illustration, see Gage (1993:ill.54)).
100. Cf. Sicard (1991:29–30; 1993:62–63).

101. Sicard (1993:62).
102. Hugh, *Moral Ark* I:III, pp. 10–12 ("Plena est omnis terra maiestate eius"); *Mystic Ark* XI, p. 160 ("Maiestas"), 161 ("Maiestatis"). Isaiah 6:3 ("plena est omnis terra gloria eius").
103. Hugh, *Moral Ark* I:III, pp. 14–16. For a discussion of the traditional exegesis on the passage from Isaiah, see Zinn (1992).
104. On the Lord embracing the world or cosmos, see Esmeijer (1978:97–100). On the iconography of Noah's Ark and related imagery, see Allen (1949), Rahner (1964:504–547), Cohn (1996), and Besseyre (1998) (which, however, I have been unable to obtain). See also Daniélou (1964:58–70) and Boblitz (1972).
105. Hugh, *Mystic Ark* XI, p. 157: "Hec ad constructionem arche his, qui plura facere aut non ualent aut nolunt, sufficere possunt. Adiecimus tamen quedam que breuiter commemorabimus."
106. Rudolph (1999, esp. pp. 21–29).
107. Rudolph (1999:23–29). This is taken up further in my forthcoming study.
108. Hugh, *Moral Ark* I:I, p. 3: "In qua collatione, quia quedam specialiter placuisse fratribus scio, ea potissimum stilo commendare uolui, non tantum ideo quod ea digna scribi existimem, quam iccirco quod quibusdam prius inaudita et ob hoc quodammodo magis grata esse cognoui."
109. Hugh, *Moral Ark* I:III, p. 17.
110. Cf. Hugh, *Moral Ark* I:III, II:I, III:XVII, IV:I, pp. 17, 33, 85, 88.
111. Hugh, *Moral Ark* I:III–V, pp. 10–32.
112. Hugh, *Moral Ark* I:III, p. 10: "Et quia hec archa Ecclesiam significat, Ecclesia autem corpus Christi est, ut euidentius exemplar tibi fiat, totam personam Christi (id est caput cum membris) in forma uisibili depinxi, ut cum totum [refers to the neuter *exemplar*, not to the feminine *persona*] uideris que deinde de parte dicuntur facilius intelligere possis."
113. Hugh, *Mystic Ark* XI, p. 162: ". . . hoc interim exemplari affectum suum prouocet."
114. Poirel (1998:15–16; 2002:132–135) also questions the trustworthiness of the method of van den Eynde.
115. Sicard (1991:30; 1993:76–99; 2001:148*–149*, 192*–195*).
116. Sicard (1993:91–99, 126–131, 133–138; 2001:9*–10*, 251*).
117. Hugh, *De sacramentis*, pref., *PL* 176:173–174.
118. Hugh, *Mystic Ark* II, X, pp. 130–131, 156. Sicard (1993:86–88, 2001:10*).
119. There is no full edition of the *Chronicon* at this time; for partial editions, see Hugh, *De tribus maximis; Chronicon* (ed. Baron); *Chronicon* (ed. Mortensen); *Chronicon* (ed. Pertz); and *Chronicon* (ed. Waitz). For further discussion of the *Chronicon*, see Baron (1967) and Zinn (1977).
120. Sicard (1993:65).
121. Hugh, *Mystic Ark* X, p. 156.
122. See above, pp. 12–14.
123. Hugh, *Mystic Ark* I, p. 123.
124. Sicard (1993:76).

125. Sicard (1993:77–80, 2001:9*–10*).
126. Hugh, *Mystic Ark* XI, pp. 157, 160.
127. Sicard (1993:77–80, 265–266).
128. Sicard (1993:77; cf. also pp. 77–80, 126–127).
129. Sicard (1993:79–80).
130. Augustine, *Ep.* 164:7–8, 187:6, v.2:526–528, v.3:85–86. Cf. Augustine, *De Genesi ad litteram* 5, 33–34, pp. 237–239, 428–432. See also Delumeau 1995:29–38 and, more broadly, Baschet 2000. The basic scriptural source for the *limbus Patrum* is Luke 16:19–31; on which see Bernstein (1993:73–74).
131. As mentioned above, p. 25, Hugh's original letter on the subject is lost. Bernard of Clairvaux, *Ep.* 77, v.7:184–200; esp. 77:11–15, pp. 192–196. Cf. Hugh, *De sacramentis* 1:10:6, *PL* 176:336–337, which, in part, quotes Bernard, *Ep.* 77:11–15; and cf. Abelard, *Sic et non* 106:2, 106:5, p. 342.
132. This structure is discussed in greater detail in my forthcoming study.
133. Hugh, *De sacramentis* 2:17, *PL* 176:597–610.
134. Hugh, *Mystic Ark* XI, p. 157: "Conus alter, qui prominet ad occidentem, habet uniuersalis resurrectionis iudicium: in dextera electos, in sinistra reprobos. In cuius coni angulo aquilonari est infernus, ubi dampnandi cum apostatibus spiritibus detrudentur."
135. Hugh, *Mystic Ark* IV, pp. 146–147. See Hugh, *De sacramentis* 1:8:1, *PL* 176:305, where, following Augustine, he notes that the first guilt of humanity was pride, and that concupiscence and ignorance are punishments for this.
136. Hugh, *Mystic Ark* XI, p. 160. Cf. Sicard (1993:80).
137. Hugh, *De sacramentis* 2:17:7–8, *PL* 176:599–600.
138. Hugh, *Mystic Ark* IX, p. 160.
139. Hugh, *Moral Ark* I:III, pp. 10–11. On Hugh's reference to Isaiah, see Zinn (1992).
140. Sicard (1993:80–81).
141. Hugh, *Mystic Ark* XI, p. 161.
142. Is. 66:1; cf. Jerome, *In Esaiam* 3:1, p. 84.
143. Hugh, *Mystic Ark* XI, p. 161.
144. See above, pp. 24–26.
145. Sicard (1993:81–84).
146. Color terminology is notoriously difficult, but the Latin word is *purpureus*, not *ruber* or some variation on its root; and Sicard's French rendering is *rouge*, which derives from *rubeus*, not *pourpre*, which derives from *purpura*. Also, see plates 7 and 8 in Sicard (1993), where two different shades of pink are used to indicate the planks and the stage or stages, contrary to the text of *The Mystic Ark*; plate 8 is comparable to figura IV in Sicard (2001), though in the latter there is now only one shade of pink.

    Elsewhere, Sicard (2001b:129) claims that the colors of the *Ark* are the same as those that Augustine gives for the buildings (*édifices*) of the City of God in *De civitate Dei* 22:24, p. 851. This is not the case. Augustine describes the colors of the sea (*maris*), not the buildings of the City of God, as changing from green to purple to blue ("... aliquando viride atque hoc multis modis, aliquando purpureum, aliquando caeruleum est"). The colors of the *Ark* are green, yellow, and purple ("uiridis, croceus, purpureus"); Hugh, *Mystic Ark* III, p. 137.

147. Hugh, *Mystic Ark* III, p. 137, "Sed ubi homines gratie interius ponuntur, purpureum oportet...."
148. Hugh, *Mystic Ark* III (second recension), p. 137: "Archa enim purpureo colore uestita est et terre superficies uiridi colore obducta."
149. Sicard (1993:83–84), citing Hugh, *Dialogus, PL* 176:32.
150. Hugh, *Mystic Ark* II, III, pp. 127–128, 132–138 (esp. pp. 132, 137–138).
151. Hugh, *Mystic Ark* III, p. 137: "Archa enim, que in superficie intrinsecus secundum diuersitatem mansionum uariis coloribus uestita est, in ea tamen parte, ubi homines naturalis legis interius collocantur, uiridi colore obduci non debet, neque croceo ubi homines scripte legis intrinsecus sunt. Sed ubi homines gratie interius ponuntur, purpureum oportet ut habeat colorem, quatenus hic solum similitudo utrunque respondeat interius, quemadmodum hominibus naturalis legis superficies terre per colorem uiridem concordat extrinsecus."
152. Hugh, *Mystic Ark* III, p. 137: "... qui in compositione arche est, sed arche similis non est..."
153. Cf. Hugh, *De sacramentis* 1:10:6, 1:10:8, *PL* 176:339, 341, among other places, where Hugh strongly makes the point that there were saved in all periods.
154. Hugh, *De tribus maximis*, p. 490. On Hugh and color, see Carruthers (1992:233–234).
155. Hugh, *Mystic Ark* III (second recension), p. 137, quoted above, p. 53.
156. Hugh, *Moral Ark* IV:IX, p. 117.
157. See above, pp. 40–45.
158. *Necrologium S. Victoris* (February 11), p. 541.
159. Sicard 1993:85.
160. Hugh, *Mystic Ark* XI, p. 159.
161. Cf. Hugh, *Moral Ark* IV:IX, p. 117, where Hugh states that there is more that could have been said.
162. See above, pp. 36–37.
163. Sicard (1993:132–133). In a later study (2001b:130), Sicard gets even more specific, stating that *The Moral Ark* was made first, with *The Mystic Ark* following eighteen months later.
164. Hugh, *Mystic Ark* II, p. 131.
165. On the dating of Bernard's letter, see the note regarding this subject in the critical edition, Bernard of Clairvaux, *Ep.* 77, v.7:184; and Luscombe 1969:26 n. 6.
166. Hugh, *Moral Ark* I:I, p. 3.

167. Sicard (1993:133–137).
168. Hugh, *Mystic Ark* X, p. 156. This suggestion is not contradicted by the papal regnancy list of the second recension, which is truncated after the second pope; *Mystic Ark* II, p. 130. On the death of Hugh, see Croydon (1939:248), who makes a convincing argument for the year being 1141 and not 1142 (cf. Squire 1962:13).
169. Sicard (1993:97–99; 2001:79*, 81*, 152*). The manuscripts are Paris, Bib. Mazarine 717 (Sicard 2001:43*) and Paris, BnF lat. 14506 (Sicard 2001:45*–46*).
170. Sicard (1993:97–98; 2001:79*, 81*).
171. Sicard (2001:192*).
172. Sicard (1993:96–97).
173. *Liber ordinis S. Victoris* 19, p. 79: "Omnes scripturae, quae in ecclesia siue intus siue foris fiunt, ad eius officium pertinent, ut ipse scriptoribus pargamena et cetera, quae ad scribendum necessaria sunt, prouideat, et eos qui pro precio scribunt, ipse conducat." On the *armarius* at Saint Victor, see Jocqué (1991:74–79).
174. Stirnemann (1990, esp. pp. 60, 72), Gasparri (1991), Jocqué (1991:74–79), Stirnemann (1991), Kaufmann (1997) (my thanks to Virginia for a copy of this article), Rouse (2000:v.1:26–27).
175. *Liber ordinis S. Victoris* 19, pp. 79–81.
176. Gasparri (1991).
177. Stirnemann (1990, esp. pp. 60, 72), Gasparri (1991), Stirnemann (1991), Kaufmann (1997).
178. Southern (1970) and esp. Southern (1982:113). For the view of Hugh within the community of Saint Victor, see the liturgical commemoration of him on the anniversary of his death in *Necrologium S. Victoris* (February 11), p. 541; for a less formal but more unusual testimony, see the *Indiculum*, briefly discussed below; on the *Indiculum*, see de Ghellinck (1910) and Bischoff (1935). Outside the abbey, the sources are too numerous to cite; but Robert of Torigny might be thought of as being representative, noting that Hugh's writings are too widely known to have to have to bother citing them; *De Immutatione* 5, *PL* 202:1313.
179. Oxford, Bodleian Library, Laud. Misc. 370 (Sicard 2001:41*); cited by Squire (1962:19).
180. Troyes, Bib. mun. 301 (Sicard 2001:48*).
181. *Indiculum*, pp. 278–279: "Et sunt capitula <* * *>." Cf. de Ghellinck (1910:276). On the headings in *The Mystic Ark*, see Sicard (2001:258*–269*).
182. On the absence of a title to the *The Mystic Ark*, see Sicard (2001:255*–258*).
183. Gasparri (1991:127–128).
184. Of eighty-eight complete, extant manuscripts of *The Mystic Ark*, only three stand alone; Sicard (2001:61*–62*).
185. Sicard (1993:105–112), including a discussion of the previous literature on this. See also Goy (1976:212–237).

186. Hugh, *Moral Ark* IV:IX, p. 117: "Breuiter dicturus eram, sed fateor uobis multa me loqui delectat. Et erat adhuc fortassis quod dicerem, si uestrum fastidium non timerem. Nunc igitur ipsius arche nostre exemplar proponamus, sicut promisimus, quod exterius depingimus, ut foris discas quid intus agere debeas, ut cum huius exemplaris formam in corde tuo expresseris domum Dei in te edificatam, esse leteris."
187. Paris, BnF lat. 14506 (Sicard 2001:45*–46*); Paris, Bib. Mazarine 717 (Sicard 2001:43*); Sicard (1993:50–51).
188. *Indiculum*, pp. 278–279.
189. This is fully analyzed by Sicard (1993:102–112).
190. Sicard (1991:29; 1993:35, 37, 39, 45, 49–52, 55–59, 64, 101–104, 106, 112; 2001:27*, 255*–258*, 271*–277*; 2001b:127, 130). This is apparently the position taken by Carruthers and Weiss, as suggested by the beginning of the translation of *The Mystic Ark* by Weiss; cf. Carruthers and Weiss (2002:45).
191. Sicard (1993:35, 37, 40–41, 56, 58). The idea that *The Mystic Ark* is a representation of the discussion found in *The Moral Ark* is followed by Carruthers and Weiss (2002:41).
192. Cf. Hugh, *Moral Ark* III, pp. 55–85 and *Mystic Ark* I, pp. 125–126.
193. Cf. Hugh, *Moral Ark* I:III, I:V, pp. 17, 31–32.
194. Bynum (1982:25–58, esp. 36–40).
195. Peter of Celle, *Ep.* 167, *PL* 202:610.
196. Hugh, *Moral Ark* I:III, I:IV, II:VIII, IV:IX, pp. 10, 15, 23, 46, 117.
197. Robert of Torigny, *De Immutatione* 5, *PL* 202:1313.
198. Guenée (1980:255); cited by Sicard (1993:96, n. 56).
199. Ferruolo (1985:22).
200. Clanchy (1997:69).
201. Sicard (1993:96, n. 56).
202. Never existed at all: Carruthers (1992:231–233, 239); Evans (1994), *passim*, but esp. p. 74; Carruthers (1998:243–246); Carruthers and Weiss (2002: 41–42). Existed only in a reduced state: Ehlers (1972:183, n. 43). Rarely produced: Sicard (1993:40–41). May or may not have existed: Zinn (1968: 136–137), Obrist (1986:36). Lecoq (1989:10), Skubiszewski (1990), Wirth (1999:392). Made, but no longer exists: Ohly (1972:100), Zinn (1972:320), Zinn (1992).
203. Manuscript illumination: Oudin (1772:1111), Hauréau (1886:91), Ehlers (1972:183, n. 43) (in a reduced state), Friedman (1985:174) (probable), Skubiszewski 1990:267, n. 11 (who sees this as one possibility), and cf. Evans (1994:75. n. 14), where he (quite rightly) chastises me and others for thinking of the *Ark* as a manuscript illumination (cf. my earlier work, Rudolph 1990:36, n. 24). Manuscript illumination, wall or floor painting, if it ever existed: Lecoq (1989:10, 21). Wall or floor painting: Gautier Dalché (1988:17). Wall painting or wall-hanging: Zinn (1992:99, n. 2). Wall-hanging: Ohly (1972:100), Wirth (1999:386)

(if it ever existed). Wall-hanging or floor painting: Sicard (1993:46, n. 72, 55). Floor painting: Kupfer (1994:269) (my thanks to Dr. Kupfer for providing me with a copy of this article), Sicard (2001b:127). Lost drawing: McGinn (1992:v.2:378). Existed, but format not discussed: Zinn (1968:137), Bronder (1972:188, 208), Zinn (1972), Esmeijer (1978:108, n. 51), Sicard (1991:29). Existed only mentally: Carruthers (1992:231–233, 239), Evans (1994), Carruthers (1998:243–246), Carruthers and Weiss (2002:41–42); cf. also Skubiszewski (1990:267, n. 11) (who sees this as one possibility).

204. Painted in front of audience: Sicard (1991:29; 1993, *passim*, but esp. pp. 34–35, 40–50; 2001:8*). *Planities*, wall-hanging, floor painting: Sicard (1993:46, n. 72, 55). Floor painting: (2001b:127). Verbal image: Sicard (1991:29; 1993, *passim*, but esp. pp. 40–42, 50–51, 54–59, 63, n. 111; 2001b:129).
205. Hugh, *Mystic Ark* II, p. 129.
206. Hugh, *Mystic Ark* XI, p. 158.
207. Hugh, *Mystic Ark* XI, p. 158.
208. Hugh, *Mystic Ark* XI, p. 159.
209. Hugh, *Mystic Ark* XI, p. 159.
210. Hugh, *Mystic Ark* XI, p. 157. Discussed above, pp. 27–28. See also p. 99, n. 196 above, which cites largely nonrhetorical references to the painting of *The Mystic Ark* in *The Moral Ark.*
211. Hugh, *Mystic Ark* I, p. 123.
212. That Hugh painted the *Ark* is clear from such repeated statements in *The Moral Ark* as, "I have depicted" (*depinxi*), "We ourselves have depicted this form" (*hanc formam nos . . . depinximus*), "To better show what we have said, we have depicted . . . We have also put on the same side . . ." (*ut melius pateant que dicimus . . . depinximus . . . in eodem latere . . . disposuimus.*); *Moral Ark* I:III, I:IV, II:VIII, pp. 10, 23, 46. This subject will be taken up further in my forthcoming study of the *Ark.*
213. On the question of what time in the canons' daily schedule the *Ark* lectures took place, see Sicard (1991:28; 1993:14–20).
214. Hugh, *Moral Ark*, *passim*, but most succinctly stated at the outset (*Moral Ark* I:I, p. 3).
215. Convenience: Hugh, *Mystic Ark* IV, pp. 140–146, 146. Descent: *Mystic Ark* IV, pp. 146–147. Ascent: *Mystic Ark* IV, V–VI, pp. 140–141, 147, 148–150, 151.
216. Hugh, *Moral Ark* I:III, p. 10. Discussed above, pp. 45–46.
217. Lehmann-Brockhaus 1955:v.5:321, "*planities,*" esp. no. 805.
218. Hugh, *Mystic Ark* I, p. 121. Discussed above, pp. 29–30. *Faciem membranae*: Hugh, *De tribus maximis*, p. 490. For the view that *planities* "can refer to any flat surface except . . . the support for a painting," see Evans (1994:76).
219. For the use of the digit as a unit of measurement by Hugh in association with the *Ark*, see *Moral Ark* I:IV, pp. 21–22.

220. My own production of the *Ark* is around 555.5 cm. (18 ft. 2 in.) high: around the height of the contemporary windows of Suger at Saint-Denis, which were meant for individual contemplation. I will discuss the issue of size more fully in my forthcoming book.

For size estimates by other scholars, see Ehlers (1972:183, n. 43), who estimates the Ark proper only, using a central cubit of 1 cm. This yields an Ark proper of 2 m in length, something he feels would have been too small for the inscriptions. While this might be true for a work of public art, it is not the case for a pedagogical work of art designed for a seminar context. Sicard (1993:55, n. 92) believes that the "Ark" would have been around 2 m in height by 1.5 m in width, though he does not specify whether he is referring to the Ark proper or to the entire painting of the *Ark*.

221. Destroyed 1943. Hahn-Woernle (1993).
222. Barber (1995:21).
223. Evans (1994). Bronder (1972:188, n. 2) rejects the idea of ekphrasis, such a rejection being implied by Lecoq (1989:10).
224. Hugh, *De vanitate* 1, pp. 29–36. For a recent study of ekphrasis, to which *The Mystic Ark* bears no relation but these passages from *De vanitate* do, see Putnam (1998, *passim*, but esp. pp. 2–3) for a discussion of the nature of ekphrasis.
225. Lifted passages: Bede, *De temporum ratione* 66, p. 464; Hugh, *Moral Ark* II:II–III, pp. 36–38; and possibly Isidore, *De natura rerum* 11, pp. 213–217; cf. Hugh, *Mystic Ark* II, VIII, XI, pp. 131–132, 153, 157–158. Mundane references to Hugh's other works: *Mystic Ark* IV, p. 143 (*De tribus diebus*); VIII, p. 153 (*Moral Ark*); X, p. 156 (a projected work on the stopping places). Separate section for inscriptions: *Mystic Ark* IV, pp. 139–140. Abbreviated nature: *Mystic Ark* XI, p. 158.
226. As a literarily simpler form than ekphrasis: Sicard (1991:29; 1993, *passim*, but esp. pp. 40–42, 50–51, 54–59, 63 n. 111; 2001b:129). Skubiszewski (1990:267, n. 11) suggests that a mental picture is one option of the text. Cf. also Zinn (1968:137). Memorization: Carruthers (1992:123, 231–239, esp. 233, 234; 1998:243–246) and Carruthers and Weiss (2002:41). On the *Ark* and memory, see also Zinn (1974b:229), Lecoq (1989:19), Sicard (1993:27–28, 60, n. 102) (where he disagrees with Carruthers that the Ark is "purely mental"), Evans (1994:75) (who criticizes Carruthers' thesis that the *Ark* is based on Ciceronian mnemonic technique), Sicard (2001b:128), and cf. Ehlers (1972:184).
227. Miscellaneous elements: Hugh, *Mystic Ark* VII, pp. 151–152. Inscriptions: *Mystic Ark* IV, pp. 139–146. Proportions: *Mystic Ark* I, p. 123.
228. Hugh, *Mystic Ark* IV, pp. 141–146, *passim*.
229. Hugh, *Moral Ark* I:III, p. 10.
230. Sicard (1993:23, 54, 96). Cf. Hugh, *Moral Ark* I:I, p. 3.
231. *Quomodo pingi debeat*, Bruxelles, Bib. roy. 4399–4402 (Sicard 2001:30*); see also Sicard (2001:256*) for only a partial listing of other, similar informal titles.

232. See Hugh, *Moral Ark* I:III, p. 10, where he describes *The Mystic Ark* as a proper work of art.
233. See above, pp. 12–14.
234. Describing the text of *The Mystic Ark* as a "step-by-step" set of instructions: Ehlers (1972:171), Zinn (1972:321), Obrist (1986:36), Sicard (1991:157, n. 219), Sicard (1993:53, n. 86, 55, 57, 58, 66), Evans (1994:74) (although he believes the painting never existed), Kupfer (1994:269), Sicard (2001b: 127).
235. The same basic procedure described in Alexander (1992:40–42) for manuscript illumination would have been applied to the wall painting of *The Mystic Ark*. Given the pedagogical nature of the painting, it seems unlikely that a fresco technique would have been used.
236. Alexander (1992:40–41). Wirth (1999:393) notes that the incorrect artistic practice described in the text of *The Mystic Ark* suggests that it is not described by a professional craftsman.
237. Cf. Hugh, *Mystic Ark* I, pp. 122–123 (central cubit), 126 (central pillar).
238. Hugh, *Moral Ark* I:I, I:III, pp. 3, 10.

BIBLIOGRAPHY

PRIMARY SOURCES

When dual systems of traditional numeration exist for primary sources, reference is made to the more precise of the two. All biblical references are to the Vulgate.

Abelard, *Sic et non*: ed. Blanche Boyer and Richard McKeon, *Sic et Non: A Critical Edition* (Chicago 1976–1977).

Ambrose, *Hexameron*: ed. Karl Schenkl, et al., *Exameron*, *CSEL* 32:1 (Vienna 1897 f.) 1–261.

Anonymus Carthusiensis, *De religionum origine*: ed. Edmond Martène, *Veterum scriptorum et monumentorum ecclesiasticorum et dogmaticorum amplissima collectio*, 9 v. (Paris 1724–1733) v.6:11–94.

Augustine, *Contra Faustum*: ed. Joseph Zycha, *Contra Faustum libri XXXIII, CSEL* 25:1 (Vienna 1891) 249–797.

Augustine, *De civitate Dei*: ed. Bernhard Dombart and Alfons Kalb, *Sancti Aurelii Augustini de civitate Dei, CCSL* 47–48 (Turnhout 1955).

Augustine, *De Genesi ad litteram*: ed. Joseph Zycha, *De Genesi ad litteram libri duodecim, CSEL* 28:1 (Vienna 1887).

Augustine, Ep.: ed. A. Goldbacher, *S. Aurelii Augustini Hipponiensis Episcopi Epistulae, CSEL* 34, 44, 57, 58 (Vienna 1895–1923).

Bede, *De temporibus*: ed. Charles W. Jones, *Bedae Vernerabilis opera* 6:3, *CCSL* 123C (Turnhout 1977) 579–611.

Bede, *De temporum ratione*: ed. Charles W. Jones, *Bedae Vernerabilis opera* 6:2, *CCSL* 123B (Turnhout 1977).

Bernard of Clairvaux, Ep.: ed. Jean Leclercq and H. M. Rochais, *Sancti Bernardi opera*, 8 v. (Rome 1957–1977), v. 7–8.

Bonaventure, *De reductione artium*: ed. by the Franciscans of Quaracchi, *Opusculum de reductione artium ad theologiam, Opera omnia*, 10 v. (1882–1902), v.5:319–325.

CCCM: Corpus Christianorum Continuatio Mediaevalis (Turnhout 1966 f.).

CCSL: Corpus Christianorum Series Latina (Turnhout 1953 f.).

CSEL: Corpus Scriptorum Ecclesiasticorum Latinorum (Vienna 1866 f.).

Honorius Augustodunensis, *De imagine mundi*: *PL* 172:115–188.

Hugh [of Saint Victor], *Adnotationes in Pentateuchon: Adnotationes elucidatoriae in Pentateuchon, PL* 175:29–86.

Hugh [of Saint Victor], *Chronicon* (ed. Baron): *Mappa mundi*, ed. Roger Baron, "Hugues de Saint-Victor lexicographe," *Cultura neolatina* 16 (1956) 137–145.

Hugh [of Saint Victor], *Chronicon* (ed. Mortensen): Lists of rulers, ed. Lars Boje Mortensen, "Hugh of St. Victor on Secular History: A Preliminary Edition of Chapters from His *Chronica* ," *Cahiers de l'institut du moyen-âge grec et latin* 62 (1992) 3–30.

Hugh [of Saint Victor], *Chronicon* (ed. Pertz): List of writers of history, ed. G. H. Pertz, "Hugonis de S. Victore Historia," *Archiv der Gesellschaft für ältere deutsche Geschichtskunde* 11 (1858) 306–308.

Hugh [of Saint Victor], *Chronicon* (ed. Waitz): List of popes and emperors, ed. Georg Waitz, "Chronica quae dicitur Hugonis de Sancto Victore," *Monumenta Germaniae Historica, Scriptores* 24, 88–97.

Hugh [of Saint Victor], *De sacramentis: De sacramentis Christianae fidei, PL* 176: 183–618.

Hugh [of Saint Victor], *Descriptio mappe mundi*: ed. Patrick Gautier Dalché, *La "Descriptio mappe mundi" de Hugues de Saint-Victor: Texte inédit avec introduction et commentaire* (Paris 1988).

Hugh [of Saint Victor], *De scripturis: De scripturis et scriptoribus sacris, PL* 175:9–28.

Hugh [of Saint Victor], *De tribus diebus*: ed. Vincenzo Liccaro, *I tre giorni dell'invisibile luce, L'union del corpo e dello spirito* (Florence 1974) 48–157.

Hugh [of Saint Victor], *De tribus maximis*: ed. William M. Green, "Hugo of St. Victor: *De tribus maximis circumstantiis gestorum* ," Speculum 18 (1943) 484–493.

Hugh [of Saint Victor], *De vanitate*: ed. Karl Müller, *Soliloquium de arrha animae und De vanitate mundi* (Bonn 1913) 26–48.

Hugh [of Saint Victor], *Dialogus: De sacramentis legis naturalis et scriptae dialogus, PL* 176:17–42.

Hugh [of Saint Victor], *Didascalicon*: ed. Charles H. Buttimer, *Hugonis de Sancto Victore Didascalicon de studio legendi*, Studies in Medieval and Renaissance Latin 10 (Washington 1939).

Hugh [of Saint Victor], *Miscellanea: Miscellanea* 1–2, *PL* 177:469–634.

Hugh [of Saint Victor], *Moral Ark*: ed. Patrice Sicard, *De archa Noe. Libellus de formatione arche, CCCM* 176 (Turnhout 2001) 1–117.

Hugh [of Saint Victor], *Mystic Ark*: ed. Patrice Sicard, *De archa Noe. Libellus de formatione arche, CCCM* 176 (Turnhout 2001) 119–162. [An English translation of *The Mystic Ark* by Jessica Weiss follows Carruthers and Weiss 2002. My own translation with extensive commentary will appear in my forthcoming study of the *Ark*.]

Hugh [of St-Victor], *Practica geometriae*: ed. Roger Baron, *Hugonis de Sancto Victore opera propaedeutica* (Notre Dame, Ind. 1966) 15–64.

Indiculum: ed. Joseph de Ghellinck, "La table des matières de la première édition des oeuvres de Hugues de Saint-Victor," *Recherches de science religieuse* 1 (1910) 270–289 and 385–396.

Isidore of Seville, *De natura rerum*: ed. Jacques Fontaine, *Traité de la nature* (Bordeaux 1960).

Isidore of Seville, *Etymologiae*: ed. W. M. Lindsay, *Etymologiarum sive Originum libri XX* (Oxford 1911).

Jerome, *In Esaiam*: ed. M. Adriaen and G. Morin, *Commentarii in Esaiam, CCSL* 73–73A, 2 v. (Turnhout 1963).

Laurence, *Ep.*: ed. Ambrogio M. Piazzoni, "Ugo di San Vittore 'auctor' delle 'Sententiae de divinitate,'" *Studi medievali* 23 (1982) 912–913.

Lehmann-Brockhaus 1955: ed. Otto Lehmann-Brockhaus, *Lateinische Schriftquellen zur Kunst in England, Wales und Schottland vom Jahre 901 bis zum Jahre 1307*, 5 v. (Munich 1955–1960).

Liber ordinis S. Victoris: ed. Luc Jocqué and Ludo Milis, *Liber ordinis Sancti Victoris Parisiensis, CCSL* 61 (Turnhout 1984).

Macrobius, *Commentarii*: ed. Iacobus Willis, *Commentarii in somnium Scipionis* (Leipzig 1963).

Martianus Capella, *De nuptiis*: ed. James Willis, *De nuptiis Philologiae et Mercurii* (Leipzig 1983).

Necrologium S. Victoris: ed. Auguste Molinier, *Obituaires de la Province de Sens* (Paris 1902–1923) v.1:531–608.

Ovid, *Metamorphoses*: ed. Moiz Haupt et al., 2 v. (Zurich 1966).

Peter of Celle, *Ep.*: *Petri Cellensis Epistolarum, PL* 202:405–636.

PL: *Patrologia latina*, ed. Jacques-Paul Migne, 221 v. (Paris 1844–1864).

Plato (trans. Chalcidius), *Timaeus*: ed. J. H. Waszink, *Timaeus: A Calcidio translatus commentarioque instructus* (London 1962).

Pliny, *Naturalis historiae*: ed. L. Jan and C. Mayhoff, *C. Plini Secundi Naturalis historiae* (repr. Stuttgart 1967).

Richard of Saint Victor, *Benjamin Maior*: *PL*:196:63–202.

Robert de Torigny, *De immutatione*: *De immutatione ordinis monachorum, PL* 202: 1309–1320.

Seneca, *Ep.*: ed. L. D. Reynolds, *L. Annaei Senecae ad Lucilium epistulae morales*, 2 v. (Oxford 1965).

Veterum scriptorum testimonia: *Veterum aliquot scriptorum de Hugone Victorino testimonia, PL* 175:CLXIII–CLXVIII.

Virgil, *Georgics*: ed. R. A. B. Mynors, *Georgics* (Oxford 1990).

Vitruvius, *De architectura*: ed. Philippe Fleury, *De l'architecture* (Paris 1990).

SECONDARY LITERATURE

Alexander 1992: Jonathan J. G. Alexander, *Medieval Illuminators and Their Methods of Work* (New Haven 1992).

Allen 1949: Don Cameron Allen, "*The Legend of Noah: Renaissance Rationalism in Art, Science and Letters*," *Illinois Studies in Language and Literature* 33:3–4 (Urbana 1949).

Barber 1995: Peter Barber, "The Evesham World Map: A Late Medieval English View of God and the World," *Imago Mundi* 47 (1995) 13–33.

Baron 1955: Roger Baron, *La contemplation et ses espèces* (Tournai 1958 [sic]) 5–40.

Baron 1957: Roger Baron, *Science et sagesse chez Hugues de Saint-Victor* (Paris 1957).

Baron 1963: Roger Baron, *Etudes sur Hugues de Saint-Victor* (Paris 1963).

Baron 1967: Roger Baron, "La Chronique de Hugues de Saint-Victor," *Studia Gratiana* 12 = *Collectanea Stephen Kuttner*, ed. J. Forchielli (1967) v.2:165–180.

Baschet 2000: Jérôme Baschet, *Le sein du père: Abraham et la paternité dans l'Occident medieval* (Paris 2000).

Bautier 1981: Robert-Henri Bautier, "Paris au temps d'Abélard," *Abélard en son temps*, Acts du Colloque international organisé à l'occasion du 9e centenaire de la naissance de Pierre Abélard (Paris 1981) 21–77.

Bautier 1991: Robert-Henri Bautier, "Les origines et les premiers développements de l'abbaye Saint-Victor de Paris," in Longère (1991:23–52).

Bernstein 1993: Alan E. Bernstein, *The Formation of Hell: Death and Retribution in the Ancient and Early Christian Worlds* (Ithaca 1993).

Besseyre 1998: Marianne Besseyre, "L'iconographie de l'arche de Noé du IIIe au XVe siècle," unpublished doctoral dissertation, Ecole des Chartes (Paris 1998).

Bischoff 1935: Bernhard Bischoff, "Aus der Schule Hugos von St. Viktor," *Beiträge zur Geschichte der Philosophie und Theologie des Mittelalters* (Aus der Geisteswelt des Mittelalters 1) supp 3:1 (Munich 1935) 246–250.

Boblitz 1972: Hartmut Boblitz, "Die Allegorese der Arche Noahs in der frühen Bibelauslegung," *Frühmittelalterliche Studien* 6 (1972) 159–170.

Bonnard 1904: Fourier Bonnard, *Histoire de l'abbaye royale et de l'ordre des chanoines réguliers de St-Victor de Paris*, 2 v. (Paris 1904).

Bronder 1972: Barbara Bronder, "Das Bild der Schöpfung und Neuschöpfung der Welt als *orbis quadratus* ," *Frühmittelalterliche Studien* 6 (1972) 188–210.

Bynum 1982: Caroline Bynum, *Jesus as Mother: Studies in the Spirituality of the High Middle Ages* (Berkeley 1982).

Carruthers 1992: Mary Carruthers, *The Book of Memory: A Study of Memory in Medieval Culture* (Cambridge 1992).

Carruthers 1998: Mary Carruthers, *The Craft of Thought: Meditation, Rhetoric, and the Making of Images, 400–1200* (Cambridge 1998).

Carruthers and Weiss 2002: Mary Carruthers and Jessica Weiss, "Hugh of St. Victor, *A Little Book About Constructing Noah's Ark* ," in ed. Mary Carruthers and Jan M. Ziolkowski, *The Medieval Craft of Memory: An Anthology of Texts and Pictures* (Philadelphia 2002), 41–45.

Châtillon 1952: Jean Châtillon, "De Guillaume de Champeaux à Thomas Gallus: Chronique d'histoire littéraire et doctrinale de l'Ecole de Saint-Victor," *Revue du moyen âge* 8 (1952), 139–162, 247–272.

Chenu 1968: Marie-Dominique Chenu, *Nature, Man, and Society in the Twelfth Century: Essays on New Theological Perspectives in the Latin West* (Chicago 1968).

Clanchy 1997: M. T. Clancy, *Abelard: A Medieval Life* (Oxford 1997).

Cohn 1996: Norman Cohn, *Noah's Flood: The Genesis Story in Western Thought* (New Haven 1996).

Croydon 1939: F. E. Croydon, "Notes on the Life of Hugh of St. Victor," *The Journal of Theological Studies* 40 (1939), 232–253.

Croydon 1950: F. E. Croydon, "Abbot Laurence of Westminster and Hugh of St. Victor," *Mediaeval and Renaissance Studies* 2 (1950), 169–171.

Daniélou 1964: Jean Daniélou, *Primitive Christian Symbols* (Baltimore 1964).

del Basso 1965: Emma del Basso, "Il De arca Noe moralia di Ugo di S. Vittore," *Atti dell'Accademia Pontaniana* 14 (1965), 219–237.

Delumeau 1995: Jean Delumeau, *History of Paradise: The Garden of Eden in Myth and Tradition* (New York 1995).

Dickinson 1950: J. C. Dickinson, *The Origins of the Austin Canons and Their Introduction into England* (London 1950).

Edson 1998: Evelyn Edson, *Mapping Time and Space: How Medieval Mapmakers Viewed Their World* (Toronto 1998).

Ehlers 1972: Joachim Ehlers, "*Arca significat ecclesiam*: Ein theologisches Weltmodell aus der ersten Hälfte des 12. Jahrhunderts," *Frühmittelalterliche Studien* 6 (1972), 171–187.

Ehlers 1973: Joachim Ehlers, *Hugo von St Viktor: Studien zum Geschichtsdenken und zur Geschichtsschreibung des 12. Jahrhunderts* (Wiesbaden 1973).

Esmeijer 1978: Anna Esmeijer, *Divina Quaternitas: A Preliminary Study in the Method and Application of Visual Exegesis* (Amsterdam 1978).

Evans 1994: Michael Evans, "Fictive Painting in Twelfth-Century Paris," *Sight and Insight: Essays on Art and Culture in Honour of E. H. Gombrich at 85*, ed. John Onians (London 1994), 73–87.

Feiss 1992: Hugh Feiss, "*Bernardus Scholasticus*: The Correspondence of Bernard of Clairvaux and Hugh of Saint Victor on Baptism," *Bernardus Magister*, ed. John Sommerfeldt (1992), 349–378.

Ferruolo 1985: Stephen C. Ferruolo, *The Origins of the University: The Schools of Paris and Their Critics, 1100–1215* (Stanford 1985).

Friedman 1985: John B. Friedman, "Les images mnémotechniques dans les manuscripts de l'époque gothique," *Jeux de mémoire: Aspects de la mnémotechnie médiévale*, ed. Bruno Roy and Paul Zumthor (Montreal 1985), 169–184.

Gage 1993: John Gage, *Color and Culture: Practice and Meaning from Antiquity to Abstraction* (Boston 1993).

Gasparri 1991: Françoise Gasparri, "'Scriptorium' et bureau d'écriture de l'abbaye Saint-Victor de Paris," in Longère (1991:119–139).

Gasparri 1996: Françoise Gasparri, "Introduction," *Suger: Oeuvres*, Les classiques de l'histoire de France au moyen âge 37 (Paris 1996).

Gasparri 2001: Françoise Gasparri, "La pensée et l'oeuvre de l'abbé Suger à la lumière de ses écrits," in Poirel (2001b:91–107).

Gautier Dalché 1988: Patrick Gautier Dalché, *La "Descriptio mappe mundi" de Hugues de Saint-Victor: Texte inédit avec introduction et commentaire* (Paris 1988).

de Ghellinck 1910: Joseph de Ghellinck, "La table des matières de la première édition des oeuvres de Hugues de Saint-Victor," *Recherches de science religieuse* 1 (1910) 270–289 and 385–396.

Goy 1976: Rudolf Goy, *Die Überlieferung der Werke Hugos von St Viktor: Ein Beitrag zur Kommunikationsgeschichte des Mittelalters* (Stuttgart 1976).

Green 1943: William M. Green, "Hugo of St. Victor: *De tribus maximis circumstantiis gestorum*," *Speculum* 18 (1943) 484–493.

Guenée 1980: Bernard Guenée, *Histoire et culture historique dans l'Occident médiéval* (Paris 1980).

Hahn-Woernle 1993: Birgit Hahn-Woernle, *Die Ebstorfer Weltkarte* (Ebstorf 1993).

Hamesse 1988: Jacqueline Hamesse, "'Collatio' et 'reportatio': Deux vocables spécifiques de la vie intellectuelle au moyen âge," *Terminologie de la vie intellectuelle au moyen âge* (Turnhout 1988) 83–87.

Häring 1982: Nikolaus M. Häring, "Commentary and Hermeneutics," *Renaissance and Renewal in the Twelfth Century*, ed. Robert L. Benson and Giles Constable (Cambridge, Mass. 1982), 173–200.

Hauréau 1886: B. Hauréau, *Les Oeuvres de Hugues de Saint-Victor: Essai critique* (Paris 1886).

Javelet 1960: Robert Javelet, "Les origins de Hugues de Saint-Victor," *Revue des sciences religieuses* 34 (1960), 74–83.

Jocqué 1991: Luc Jocqué, "Les structures de la population claustrale dans l'order de Saint-Victor au XIIe siècle: Un essai d'analyse du 'Liber ordinis,'" in Longère (1991:53–95).

Kaufmann 1997: Virginia Roehrig Kaufmann, "The Halberstadt Glossed Mark, Parisian Book Painting of the 1130s to the 1150s, and the Augustinian Abbey of St. Victor," *Königtum und Kirche als Kulturträger im östlichen Harzvorland*, Abhandlungen der Sächsischen Akademie der Wissenschaften zu Leipzig, Philologisch-historische Klasse 74:2 (Berlin 1997), 144–186.

Lecoq 1989: Danielle Lecoq, "La 'Mappemonde' du *De arca Noe mystica* de Hugues de Saint-Victor (1128–1129)," *Géographie du monde au moyen âge et à la renaissance*, ed. Monique Pelletier (Paris 1989), 9–31.

Lehmann-Brockhaus 1955: See *Primary Sources.*

Longère 1991: ed. Jean Longère, *L'abbaye Parisienne de Saint-Victor au moyen âge*, Bibliotheca Victorina 1 (Paris 1991).

Lottin 1958: Odon Lottin, "Quelques recueils d'écrits attribués à Hugues de Saint-Victor," *Recherches de théologie ancienne et médiévale* 25 (1958), 248–284.

Luscombe 1969: D. E. Luscombe, *The School of Peter Abelard: The Influence of Abelard's Thought in the Early Scholastic Period* (Cambridge 1969).

McGinn 1992: Bernard McGinn, *The Presence of God: A History of Western Christian Mysticism*, 2 v. (New York 1992–1994).

Mietke 1972: Jürgen Mietke, "Zur Herkunft Hugos von St. Viktor," *Archiv für Kulturgeschichte* 54 (1972), 241–265.

Obrist 1986: Barbara Obrist, "Image et Prophétie au XIIe siècle: Hugues de Saint-Victor et Joachim de Flore," *Mélanges de l'Ecole Française de Rome* 98 (1986), 35–63.

Ohly 1972: Friedrich Ohly, "Die Kathedral als Zeitenraum: Zum Dom von Siena," *Frühmittelalterliche Studien* 6 (1972) 94–158.

Oudin 1772: Casimir Oudin, *Commentarius de scriptoribus Ecclesiae antiquis*, 3 v. (Leipzig 1772).

Piazzoni 1982: Ambrogio M. Piazzoni, "Ugo di San Vittore 'auctor' delle 'Sententiae de divinitate,'" *Studi medievali* ser. 3, 23 (1982), 861–911.

Poirel 1998: Dominique Poirel, *Hugues de Saint-Victor* (Paris 1998).

Poirel 1998b: Dominique Poirel, "L'école de Saint-Victor au moyen âge: Bilan d'un demi-siècle historiographique," *Bibliotheque de l'Ecole des Chartes* 156 (1998), 187–205.

Poirel 2001: Dominique Poirel, "*Symbolice et anagogice*: L'école de Saint-Victor et la naissance du style gothique," in Poirel (2001b:141–170).

Poirel 2001b: ed. Dominique Poirel, *L'abbé Suger, le manifeste gothique de Saint-Denis et la pensée victorine*, Rencontres médiévales européennes 1 (Turnhout 2001).

Poirel 2002: Dominique Poirel, *Livre de la nature et débat trinitaire au XIIe siècle: Le "De tribus diebus" de Hugues de Saint-Victor* (Turnhout 2002).

Pollitt 1966: H. P. Pollitt, "Considerations on the Structure and Sources of Hugh of St Victor's Notes on the Octateuch," *Recherches de théologie ancienne et médiévale* 33 (1966), 5–38.

Putnam 1998: Michael C. J. Putnam, *Virgil's Epic Designs: Ekphrasis in the Aeneid* (New Haven 1998).

Rahner 1964: Hugo Rahner, *Symbole der Kirche: Die Ekklesiologie der Väter* (Salzburg 1964).

Rouse 2000: Richard H. Rouse and Mary A. Rouse, *Illiterati et uxorati. Manuscripts and Their Makers: Commercial Book Producers in Medieval Paris 1200–1500*, 2 v. (Turnhout 2000).

Rudolph 1990: Conrad Rudolph, *Artistic Change at St-Denis: Abbot Suger's Program and the Early Twelfth-Century Controversy over Art* (Princeton 1990).

Rudolph 1999: Conrad Rudolph, "In the Beginning: Theories and Images of Creation in Northern Europe in the Twelfth Century," *Art History* 22 (1999), 3–55.

Schneider 1933: Wilhelm A. Schneider, *Geschichte und Geschichtsphilosophie bei Hugo von St Victor: Ein Beitrag zur Geistegeschichte des 12. Jahrhunderts*, Münstersche Beiträge zur Geschichtsforschung 3:2 (Munich 1933).

Schneyer 1964: J. B. Schneyer, "Ergänzungen der Sermones und Miscellanea des Hugo von Sankt Viktor aus verschiedenen Handschriften" *Recherches de théologie ancienne et médiévale* 31 (1964), 260–286.

Sicard 1991: Patrice Sicard, *Hugues de Saint-Victor et son école* (Turnhout 1991).

Sicard 1993: Patrice Sicard, *Diagrammes médiévaux et exégèse visuelle: Le Libellus de formatione arche de Hugues de Saint-Victor* (Paris 1993).

Sicard 2001: Patrice Sicard, introduction to *De archa Noe. Libellus de formatione arche, CCCM* 176 (Turnhout 2001) 7*–287*.

Sicard 2001b: Patrice Sicard, "L'urbanisme de la Cité de Dieu: Constructions et architectures dans la pensée théologique du XIIe siècle," in (Poirel 2001b:109–140).

Skubiszewski 1990: Piotr Skubiszewski, "L'intellectuel et l'artiste face à l'oeuvre à l'époque romane," *Le travail au moyen âge: Une approche interdisciplinaire*, Publications de l'Institut d'études médiévales 10 (1990), 263–321.

Smalley 1952: Beryl Smalley, *The Study of the Bible in the Middle Ages* (Oxford 1952).

Southern 1970: R. W. Southern, "Humanism and the School of Chartres," *Medieval Humanism and Other Studies* (Oxford 1970), 61–85.

Southern 1982: R. W. Southern, "The Schools of Paris and the School of Chartres,"

Renaissance and Renewal in the Twelfth Century, ed. Robert L. Benson and Giles Constable (Cambridge, Mass. 1982), 113–137.

Squire 1962: Aelred Squire, "Introduction," *Hugh of Saint-Victor: Selected Spiritual Writings*, trans. by a Religious of C.S.M.V. (London 1962), 13–42.

Stirnemann 1990: Patricia Stirnemann, "Fils de la vierge: L'initiale à filagrannes parisienne, 1140–1314," *Revue de l'art* 90 (1990), 58–73.

Stirnemann 1991: Patricia Stirnemann, "La production manuscrite et la bibliothèque de Saint-Victor 1140–1155," in Longére (1991:140–141).

Taylor 1957: Jerome Taylor, *The Origin and Early Life of Hugh of St Victor: An Evaluation of the Tradition*, Texts and Studies in the History of Mediaeval Education 5 (Notre Dame, Ind. 1957).

Van den Eynde 1960: Damien Van den Eynde, *Essai sur la succession et la date des écrits de Hugues de Saint-Victor*, Spicilegium Pontificii Athenaei Antoniani 13 (Rome 1960).

Weisweiler 1949: Heinrich Weisweiler, "Die Arbeitsmethode Hugos von St. Viktor: Ein Beitrag zum Entstehen seines Hauptwerkes *De sacramentis*," *Scholastik* 20–24 (1949), 59–87, 232–267.

Wirth 1999: Jean Wirth, *L'image à l'époque romane* (Paris 1999).

Zinn 1968: Grover Zinn, "History and Contemplation: The Dimensions of the Restoration of Man in Two Treatises on the Ark of Noah by Hugh of St Victor," unpublished doctoral dissertation, Duke University (Durham, N.C. 1968).

Zinn 1971: Grover Zinn, "Hugh of St. Victor and the Ark of Noah: A New Look," *Church History* 40 (1971), 261–272.

Zinn 1972: Grover Zinn, "Mandala Symbolism and Use in the Mysticism of Hugh of St. Victor," *History of Religions* 12 (1972–1973), 317–341.

Zinn 1974: Grover Zinn, "'*Historia fundamentum est*': The Role of History in the Contemplative Life According to Hugh of St. Victor," *Contemporary Reflections on the Mediaeval Christian Traditions: Essays in Honor of Ray C. Petry* (Durham, N.C. 1974), 135–158.

Zinn 1974b: Grover Zinn, "Hugh of Saint Victor and the Art of Memory," *Viator* 5 (1974), 211–234.

Zinn 1975: Grover Zinn, "*De gradibus ascensionum*: The Stages of Contemplative Ascent in Two Treatises on Noah's Ark by Hugh of St. Victor," *Studies in Medieval Culture* 5 (1975), 61–79.

Zinn 1977: Grover Zinn, "The Influence of Hugh of St. Victor's *Chronicon* on the *Abbreviationes Chronicorum* by Ralph of Diceto," *Speculum* 52 (1977), 38–61.

Zinn 1992: Grover Zinn, "Hugh of St Victor, Isaiah's Vision, and *De arca noe*," *Studies in Church History* 28 (1992), 99–116.

INDEX

www.ingramcontent.com/pod-product-compliance
Lightning Source LLC
LaVergne TN
LVHW081601100826
845153LV00004B/428

* 9 7 8 0 8 7 1 6 9 9 4 4 2 *